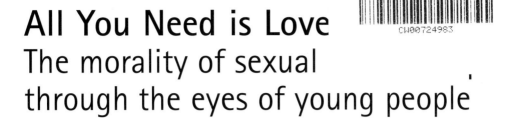

All You Need is Love

The morality of sexual
through the eyes of young people

Sue Sharpe and Rachel Thomson

national
children's
bureau
making a difference

NCB promotes the voices, interests and well-being of all children and young people across every aspect of their lives.

As an umbrella body for the children's sector in England and Northern Ireland, NCB provides essential information on policy, research and best practice for its members and other partners.

NCB aims to:
- challenge disadvantage in childhood
- work with children and young people to ensure they are involved in all matters that affect their lives
- promote multidisciplinary cross-agency partnerships and good practice
- influence government policy through policy development and advocacy
- undertake high quality research and work from an evidence-based perspective
- disseminate information to all those working with children and young people, and to children and young people themselves.

NCB has adopted and works within the UN Convention on the Rights of the Child.

Published by the National Children's Bureau

National Children's Bureau, 8 Wakley Street, London EC1V 7QE
Tel: 020 7843 6000
Website: www.ncb.org.uk
Registered charity number: 258825

© National Children's Bureau 2005

ISBN 1 904787 35 5

British Library Cataloguing in Publication Data
A catalogue record for this book is available from the British Library

The views expressed in this publication are those of the authors, and do not necessarily reflect those of the publisher

All rights reserved. No part of this publication may be reproduced, stored in a retrieval system or transmitted in any form by any person without the written permission of the publisher.

Cover by JVT Design
Typesetting by Curran Publishing Services, Norwich
Manufactured in the EU by L.P.P.S. Ltd, Wellingborough

Contents

About the authors

Sue Sharpe is a freelance social researcher whose research interests have mainly been the lives and experiences of young people, but have also involved family life, motherhood, and men's health. She has published various other books based on research with young people. Her current work includes a longitudinal study of youth transitions based at London South Bank University, where she is a Visiting Fellow.

Rachel Thomson is Lecturer in Children and Young People in the School of Health and Social Welfare at the Open University. She has been involved in research around young people, sexuality, values and identities since 1998 and has published widely in these areas. Her most recent project is a study of motherhood as a changing social identity.

Acknowledgements

The research on which this 'thinkpiece' is based was a collective endeavour involving Sue Sharpe and Rachel Thomson, Sheila Henderson, Janet Holland, and Sheena McGrellis. Simon Blake provided editorial support and contributed to the concluding Section Five.

1. Introduction

A brief glance at the Sunday newspapers shows you that there is a lot of anxiety about sexual morality. Yet, at the same time, a great deal of entertainment is made from reporting the sexual antics of the famous and increasingly not so famous – what has been described as a very British 'naughty but nice' approach to sexual morality (Epstein and Johnson 1998). The most anxious of the coverage in our media concerns the sexuality of young people – be it concerns about sex and relationships education 'putting ideas into children's heads', 'gym slip mums', sexual harassment in the primary school, or sexual abuse.

There are legitimate reasons to worry about the sexualisation of children and young people. There are certainly adults who wish to exploit children sexually. There are also businesses and corporations who understand that sexualised images of children and young people are a powerful marketing tool. The desire to protect children and young people from adult sexuality becomes focused around their access to information and images – played out in controversies over the internet, the contents of young women's magazines, and the contents of sex and relationships education curricula. Sue Scott and colleagues (1998) suggest that in contemporary society children become the bearers of a generalised risk anxiety, which is sexualised and fed back to children in the form of the 'idea that sexuality *per se* is inimical to children's well being'. From this perspective they suggest that childhood is seen to be 'at risk from pressures towards early maturity, conspicuous consumption and precocious sexuality', a concern that in turn legitimises moves to deny children knowledge about sex.

However, we also recognise that sexuality is a legitimate part of childhood and youth. For example, most parents are prepared to discuss 'where babies come from' with their children even if they find it difficult or embarrassing. They may also explain that bodies can be a source of pleasure, that bodily explorations and passionate attachments will be a part of growing up. It is not that we don't recognise the potential for children and young people to be sexual, it is that we are concerned to protect them from a sexuality constructed from the position of the adult.

What complicates the picture is that the boundary between adulthood and youth is increasingly unclear. In the past, the different markers of adulthood were relatively coterminous – with economic independence, leaving home and establishing a sexual relationship happening at roughly the same time. Now we increasingly find a fragmentation in the markers of adulthood, with some accessed earlier (such as independent consumption) and others accessed later (such as economic independence). In this process, sexual activity has become one of the more accessible forms of being 'grown up' available to young people. Moore and Rosenthal (1998) suggest that what they term 'sexual initiation' has become 'the *rite de passage* of modern adolescents' providing 'an opportunity to move to adult roles that are substantially delayed for them in other areas such as career choice and economic independence'.

Consistent with this picture, we find that the age at which young people first have a sexual experience has been falling and that the gender gap (where young men had sex earlier) is closing. What is also worth noting is that although 'sexual competence' (feelings of efficacy, lack of regret and so forth) tends to increase with age, the trend towards having sex earlier is also associated with rising levels of sexual competence (Johnson and others 1994, Wellings and others 2001). So what we may be witnessing is a picture in which sexual relationships are becoming an increasingly important marker of early adulthood, and that young people invest these relationships with importance and seek to exercise maturity in and through them.

In the context of such significant demographic, technological and cultural shifts, it is little surprise that there is such anxiety about the sexuality of the young and that these debates are located within wider moral stories of decline and a loss of innocence. Yet these are very much adult debates, which leave very little room for young people themselves. How much do we know about young people's sexual values? Where and how do they draw lines between right and wrong, acceptable and unacceptable? What are the issues that provoke debate among them? Despite mountains of research into young people's sexual behaviour and risk-taking, these are questions that we have mostly forgotten to ask.

This 'thinkpiece' is about the morality of sexual relationships as seen through the eyes of young people. It is based on the responses of 11- to 16-year-olds participating in a project on moral values, called The Respect Study, in which they answered questions or discussed statements on a wide-ranging set of issues via a questionnaire, focus groups, and individual in-depth interviews. Because of the young people's age and relative sexual inexperience, and because the main focus of the study did not include sexual practice, there was little discussion of sexual practice itself. However, we did ask young people what they *thought* and *felt* about sex, including: under-age sex and the age of consent laws; sexual pressures; teenage pregnancy; abortion; pornography; being able to support a child; and the factors that make sex legitimate. These and other issues are explored in this thinkpiece, and illustrated through the voices of the young people themselves.[1]

A brief look back

Out of the first half of the 20th century in Britain, which had included two World Wars, there emerged a society more eager and willing to embrace social changes. These included aspects related to sexuality, such as contraception, abortion, homosexuality and divorce. Since then, and especially over the last few decades, there has been an increasing amount of sexuality in the public domain and also in young people's lives. By the 1970s, ideas about love, sex and marriage were already experiencing even more change, fuelled by the apparent liberalisation of sexuality. The most obvious feature of this was the uncoupling of sex from marriage and reproduction, and from marital monogamy in the 1960s and '70s (Hawkes 1999). One crucial element of this was the development of the contraceptive pill. Until this point, marital sex had been seen as the only 'respectable' sex. But this secure sexual framework was already being challenged with the improvements in the economy and an increasing demand for labour, which was being taken up by women. Young people were also benefiting from the relatively full employment opportunities that offered them an independent income and, therefore, some earlier independence from their parents and the constraints of the parental home. An autonomous teenage subculture had been developing in the moral and material space that had opened up between the generations at this time. Young people suddenly came into view as a 'social problem'. The initial restriction of prescribed contraception to married women was lifted by the early 1970s. This helped to ward off the threat of pregnancy provided by the increase in extra-marital sex being enjoyed by a subculture of economically independent young people. Although there appeared to be such a

---

1   The names of the young people have been changed to preserve anonymity.

liberalising of sexuality, this loosening of the moral framework did not include homosexuality, which continued to be marginalised.

The various legal Acts in the 1960s and 1970s that focused on divorce, pornography, homosexuality, and contraception and abortion, appeared to go some way towards promoting liberal moral values, while at the same time helping to prevent what could be seen as the worst consequences of the trends at the time, such as unwanted pregnancies and illegal abortions. In 1967, both abortion and homosexuality found increased legitimisation in Acts of parliament. The effect of the Divorce Reform Act (1971) and the Matrimonial Causes Act (1973) was to make divorce much easier to obtain. This reinforced and reflected the loosening of strict attitudes towards divorce.

There have been a number of other important developments that have made significant contributions to young people and their sexual lives and futures. As already said, the development of contraception served to revolutionise women's lives from the 1960s onwards, by separating sex and reproduction, and now its many forms are taken for granted by young people today. Gradually, attitudes to having children outside marriage and through teenage pregnancy have softened. This may not be totally approved of in all areas of society, but many women, either cohabiting or without a partner, now have children, and teenage pregnancy is seen as more of a worry than a stigma. Teenage pregnancy had not necessarily been seen previously as bad if it was contained safely within marriage, but with the increase in opportunities for girls' education, and their own rising expectations, early marriage and pregnancy has become seen as a career disadvantage for (especially middle-class) young women. Pregnancy in under-16-year-olds has always caused moral and physical concern and obviously marriage is not legally possible at this age.

The softening in strict attitudes to sexuality has been facilitated somewhat by the reduction in power and influence of the church, and religion in general. It has been further fuelled by the increased visibility of sex in the public arena – in the media and in the public lives of celebrities and politicians. Nowadays everyone can read about the private sexual lives of famous people in graphic detail in the papers and magazines, and watch it on the visual media. It is part of an increasing marketing of sex for consumption. Within schools, the increase and improvement in sex and relationships education has had a chequered history. There is clearly more and more need to inform young people about sex; educate them about contraception and protect them from infections through safe sex; and make space for informed and comfortable discussion about sexual relationships.

The Respect Study

Talking about social change inevitably involves a discussion of values, that is, the extent to which changes can be understood in terms of progress, decline or a combination of the two. Too often such discussions exclude the voices of young people. This exploration of young people's sexual values is based largely around some of the responses of young people from England and Northern Ireland who took part in a study of moral values during 1997–1999. It was called The Respect Study.

The Respect Study was a project commissioned by the Economic and Social Research Council in 1996 (entitled 'Youth values: identity, diversity and social change', www.lsbu.ac.uk/fhss/ff/). It was a major study involving over 1700 young people aged 11–16 and used a range of methods to generate rich data about the lives, loves, hopes and fears of young people growing up in the UK today. The authors of this thinkpiece were part of The Respect Study research team and our aim was to understand more about the relationships between what young people value, their identities and their social environments. As part of this, we examined how young people understand the processes of their own moral development and how they deal with different contemporary values. We explored the part played by age, gender, ethnicity, religion, social class, and type of family and the vital contributions of location, place and community in the construction of young people's moral identity. The research was made particularly interesting through being carried out in schools in five contrasting locations: a city in Northern Ireland; inner-city London; a Home Counties commuter belt town; a rural village; and a deprived estate in the North of England.

The main methods that produced the material referred to here were: an extensive questionnaire to all participants; and focus groups made up from those who had volunteered to take part in discussing issues raised in, or as a by-product of, the questionnaires. Some information was also given within in-depth interviews carried out with a small sample from each school. We also held a number of extra focus groups, including a gay and lesbian group, whose members were slightly older (mainly 17- to 18-year-olds). (More detailed information about the questionnaire results of this research can be found in *Through the moral maze* by McGrellis and others (2000, www.lsbu.ac.uk/fhss/ff).)

The young people taking part in The Respect Study were not asked about sexuality in terms of actual sexual activities or sexual pleasure, but various moral issues around sexuality were explored through some of the 'contentious statements' used to provoke discussion in many of the focus groups. These issues also came up during some of the individual interviews. Looking over many of the responses relating to sexuality, it is the young women who more frequently talk, and have more to say, about this. This is not surprising since it is women whose lives have been more obviously affected by changes in things like contraception and abortion, and whose daily lives are more likely to be affected by gaining a sexual reputation. Young men are somewhat less forthcoming, possibly because they are less practised or articulate about these matters. Young women are more used to discussing more intimate issues as well as the lives of characters portrayed in soap operas. Conversation, especially among male peers, tends to be more restricted to less personal subjects like sport, or if it is related to sex, it is stories about supposed sexual success and performance (Holland and others 1993; 1998). Consequently, there are slightly more young women quoted here than young men.

The Respect Study made a point of comparing various locations, and one of these was Northern Ireland, where four schools of varying religious predominance (Catholic, Protestant, or mixed) took part. In the historical and current context of religious conflict in this area, young people living there face a rather different social and political reality from that in England, and the impact of this can be seen in many of their values, attitudes and expectations.

2. Patterns in sexual values

We begin by exploring the overall shape of young people's sexual values by drawing on an analysis of their responses to the questionnaire part of the study. The advantage of using this kind of research tool is that it enables us to compare the responses of young people across the sample and to identify structures and patterns within young people's responses. By 'structures' we mean that there may be underlying logic to the way in which young people respond to different moral questions – for example, a person who thinks that euthanasia could be morally acceptable may also be more likely to think that abortion is morally acceptable. By 'patterns' we mean that these logics may differ according to factors such as age, gender, locality, religion and ethnicity.

In order to identify these structures and patterns, we carried out a factor analysis of young people's responses to a list of 48 ethical issues. They were invited to indicate their view as to whether each item was always, usually, sometimes, rarely or never wrong. Clearly this is a crude method, which misses the subtleties of ethical deliberation and meaning making, and we have balanced the findings with a range of other more qualitative approaches to understanding young people's moral views. These are also reported in this thinkpiece. What we did find from the factor analysis was that a number of dimensions emerged that reflected an underlying structure to young people's values. What is of particular interest here is that many (but importantly not all) of those items relating to sexuality and sexual behaviour fell within what we have called a 'sexual values' factor.[2] The items included in this factor can be seen in Figure 2.1.

---

2   Although this only accounted for a relatively small amount of the total variance (3 per cent), this cluster of issues hung together in an important and coherent way.

> ### Figure 2.1 Sexual values factor
> Watching or reading pornography
>
> Pressurising someone to have sex
>
> Prostitution
>
> Sexism
>
> Unsafe sex

Overall, the majority of the young people tended to endorse disapproval of all these items. Young women of all ages and across all schools were more disapproving than were young men. This gender difference was greatest in the higher ages: whereas 62 per cent and 64 per cent of young women in Year 10 and Year 11 respectively responded more disapprovingly on this factor of sexual values, the relative proportions for young men of these ages was 26 per cent and 30 per cent. Young people from Northern Ireland were more disapproving than those from England; and such attitudes were also shown by those young people who were more pro-authority,[3] and by those who belonged to a religion or defined themselves as being 'religious'.

Other sexual or relationship issues fell *outside* the 'sexual values' factor but within the patterns of other values. For example, attitudes towards 'sex under 16 years' fell within what we called the 'illicit conventions' factor (Figure 2.2). This item was distinguished by various class differences, with middle-class young people being less approving than those from the working class.

> ### Figure 2.2 Illicit conventions factor
> Using violence in self-defence
>
> Carrying a weapon
>
> Drinking alcohol
>
> Taking revenge
>
> Fighting
>
> Sexual intercourse under the age of 16
>
> Graffiti/spray-painting

---

3   Young people who answered a certain set of attitudinal questions were given a score that reflected their orientation to authority. On the whole, young people in this study were favourably orientated towards authority (52 per cent pro-authority; 6 per cent anti-authority; and 42 per cent in the middle range). Those who were most opposed to authority, as measured by this scale, tended to be male, older and working class.

Attitudes towards abortion fell into a pattern of response with other 'life issues', which included euthanasia, cloning and suicide (Figure 2.3). There were no significant gender differences here, but working-class young people were less approving than middle-class.

Figure 2.3 Life issues factor

Suicide

Abortion

Euthanasia

Cloning animals

Attitudes towards divorce and two-timing fell into what we called a 'trust and interpersonal values' factor (Figure 2.4). These related more specifically to strengths of feeling around friendships and relationships, something especially prominent in Years 7 and 8, and although in interviews these seemed more important for young women, there were no significant gender differences here.

Figure 2.4 Trust and interpersonal values factor

Calling people names

Two-timing

Lying to your parents

Divorce

So how can we interpret these patterns? The first factor, that of sexual values, is most clearly structured by age and gender. Thus young people tend to become somewhat less disapproving of these items with age. However, there is also a significant gender gap which becomes more pronounced with age. These differences hold even when, for example, social class, locality and religion are controlled for. These are the issues that young men and women disagree about, and which it could be argued play an important part in the construction of masculine and feminine identities.

Views on other items were less distinguished by gender and more distinguished by social class. Thus sex under the age of 16 was more acceptable to working-class young people, whilst abortion was more acceptable to middle-class young people.

These findings are consistent with what we know about behaviour, which is that the age of sexual initiation is lower for people from the working class and that abortion is more likely to be taken up by the middle classes. It also alerts us to the possibility that sexual cultures may be highly localised. We have explored this elsewhere and found striking differences between the sexual values of young people living in different communities with, for example, sexual experience and parenthood considered to be a sign of 'maturity' in one economically deprived housing estate and a sign of 'immaturity' in an affluent home counties commuter town (Thomson 2000). Within each community, there exist distinct moral economies – within which sexuality and parenthood have meaning – which are, in turn, shaped by economic and educational opportunities. Within these local moral economies, young people's decisions about the sequencing of adulthood have their own logic. Therefore it 'makes sense' for one young woman to enter parenthood in her teens as a first stage towards acquiring responsibility and some authority within her community. Likewise, it 'makes sense' for another to defer the complications of heterosexual attractions and sexual relationships until she has managed to secure her entry into higher education.

One sex-related item did not fit into any of the factors – homosexuality. The pattern of young people's responses to this item reflects the centrality of homosexuality as an issue that produces conflict, uncertainty and reaction among young people (and adults). The questionnaire item asked the young people to judge 'Homosexuality (lesbian/gay)'. The verdict of these young people on this issue was polarised – either they tended to endorse 'always wrong' or 'never wrong', with relatively low proportions for the intermediate categories. The responses also varied significantly by gender. In general, the young people's responses to questions relating to sexual practices and values (for example, under-age sex, prostitution) followed a pattern, showing young women less approving than young men. Attitudes to homosexuality stood out as contradicting this. The girls took a much more liberal stance than did the boys (see Table 2.1). More than two out of five (42 per cent) of the boys considered that homosexuality was 'always wrong', and one in five (21 per cent) thought that it was 'never wrong'. The pattern of the girls' responses was in the opposite direction. Only 18 per cent endorsed 'always wrong', and 36 per cent considered that it was 'never wrong'. Therefore not only do both the boys and girls tend to be somewhat polarised in their views, but the majority in each case tends to lean towards opposite ends of the scale. Boys' homophobia has frequently been described so this is not an unexpected result, but it does highlight the different ground that boys and girls inhabit on this issue (see also Sharpe 2002).

Table 2.1 Young people's judgements about 'homosexuality'

	Always wrong		Usually wrong		Sometimes wrong		Rarely wrong		Never wrong		Not sure	
	%	N	%	N	%	N	%	N	%	N	%	N
Boys	42	366	8	72	8	68	8	68	21	184	10	86
Girls	18	146	8	69	11	92	15	120	36	287	9	72

Looking at patterns for different ages, the girls showed a slight liberalisation of judgement with increasing age. For the boys, however, there appeared to be little movement in their generally negative attitudes and, if anything, these seemed to get rather more entrenched with age. Higher levels of disapproval were also associated with a number of other factors, such as belonging to a Protestant religion; coming from a working-class background; having parents who were 'very strict'; being black or Asian; having an anti-authority orientation; and living in Northern Ireland. Attitudes varied according to location, for example the young people in the London school appeared to have the most negative views, possibly this was related to the relatively strict ethnic and religious backgrounds of many of them, and the most liberal attitudes were expressed in the two rural English schools. Such a mixed response must be set against an overall trend towards increased liberality and may, in fact, reflect the uneven and tumultuous effect of the liberalising process in action. (The young people's views on homosexuality are explored in more detail in *Debating sexual values*, page 43.)

Young people's sexual cultures are clearly important in providing a context to their views, and there are mismatches between the values they espouse (or even tick in a questionnaire) and their lived sexual cultures. In the rest of this thinkpiece we will explore the other data sources we generated so as to put some flesh on the 'bones' provided by the questionnaire responses.

3. Making sex legitimate

In this section we explore one of the strongest themes that emerged from the focus groups of young people, namely the conditions, characteristics and circumstances that make sex legitimate – put crudely, that distinguishes 'good sex' from 'bad sex'. These focus-group discussions were structured around a number of contentious statements, which we generated in part through an analysis of young people's questionnaire responses and in part through picking up on the themes that characterise discussion of teenage sexuality in popular discourse. The statements most relevant to this section focus on consent and the limits of choice, namely:

- You should only have sex if you love someone.
- If a girl says no to sex she doesn't really mean it.
- The age of consent for sex should be lowered to 14.

Before embarking on an analysis of the different views that young people express on these questions, it is first worth considering *why* this is an area of heightened debate among young people. As we discussed in the introduction, sexual practices and norms have changed considerably over a generation. In the past, there was some certainty (if not total conformity) in relation to the factors that make sex morally legitimate – marriage and procreation. The arrival of accessible contraception opened up a space between sex and procreation, a space that was filled by a range of voices including those of feminists, medics, hedonists and others who argued that sex might be for pleasure, self-knowledge, even health. The progressive fall in the age of sexual initiation, alongside an increase in the age of marriage and childbearing, suggests that the traditional legitimisation of sex through the institution of marriage and the church is no longer as authoritative as in the past. Yet it is not clear that this single source of authority has been replaced. Rather, it appears that there is a range of competing discourses or 'regimes' which provide a framework for legitimating sex, and within which distinctions between good sex and bad sex can be made. So it may be that this is an area of debate precisely because a number of different values regimes come into conflict. It may also be that there are some underlying tensions that can be contested in different ways within them.

So what are the values regimes that characterise young people's discussions about when it is legitimate to have sex? We have identified the following from an analysis of our data:

■ Romance: Sex as legitimised by love

■ Play: Sex as legitimised by pleasure

■ Security: Sex as legitimised by commitment

■ Equity: Sex as legitimised by consent

■ Legality: Sex as legitimised by the law

■ Safety: Sex as legitimised by its consequences

Through an illustration of these themes we hope to show three things. First, that young people move easily between different values regimes in their discussions, suggesting that there is no single source of moral authority that shapes their views. Second, that these values regimes are positioned very differently with regard to wider structures of power, and that some are more 'private/informal' and others more 'public/formal'. Third, that questions of gender difference are central to young people's discussions, whatever values regime is invoked.

Romance: Sex as legitimised by love

Interviewer:	When do you think it's the right thing to do – to have sex with somebody?
Donna:	When you're over age and you've got a proper boyfriend that you know you can trust.
Interviewer:	You love him?
Donna & Sonia:	Yeah.
Interviewer:	Do you think love is important in that?
Donna & Sonia:	Yeah.
Interviewer:	And when you say 'love' what does that mean?
Donna:	Caring for each other and not going to go around saying, oh, guess what? And then finishing with them and you just get called.

aged 14 to 15, in London

> I'm not gonna have sex unless it's for the right, the right moment that you
> really think you – really, really wanna get close to your boyfriend then –
> I think that's the right time.
> *Estelle, aged 14*

Many of the young people in The Respect Study felt that there was a 'right time'
for sex, and preferably with the 'right' person. They also thought, or at least
hoped, that they would instinctively recognise this time, and person. Perhaps this
is part of the romanticism of sexual relationships, which is fuelled in much of the
media where the hero and heroine finally fall happily into each other's arms, and
hence into bed. In real life, of course, this situation may turn out quite differently,
or creates more problems than it solves. This kind of romanticism was reflected in
one of the statements discussed by the young people in their groups, which
contended that: 'You should only have sex if you love someone'. It produced a
variety of responses, but in general, the young people tended to agree rather than
disagree with this assertion. This was accentuated by the younger age groups, by
young women, and those young people living in Northern Ireland where the
influence of both Catholic and Protestant religions tended to teach 'no sex before
marriage', even if this was often transgressed. Some of those in the study, from
ethnic groups such as Turkish and Asian, were also more strictly regulated in this
respect by the moral codes of their religions, and their responses were shaped by
these expectations.

This statement produced a gendered response, with young women emphasising
love as being a more important criterion than the young men. This has also
been found in other studies, such as the research on young women's and young
men's negotiation of sexual relationships (Women Risk and AIDS Project
(WRAP) and Men, Risk and AIDS Project (MRAP), Holland and others 1998).
Adopting different languages of sex and love is a crucial mechanism in the
constitution of gender within heterosexuality. Holland and others noted that
metaphors of battle and conquest dominate the way young men talk about their
experiences in the male peer group. Within this, they conspire to 'take sex' from
women. This language of 'robbery' stands in opposition to a more feminine
language of sex as love and commitment. For men, falling in love puts them in
danger of being trapped by a woman. For 16-year-old Paul, love meant
something lasting for the rest of life, and this can be quite scary for many young
men to contemplate.

> Paul: Being in love? – you want to stay with them for the rest
>   of your life just – becomes part of you.

| Interviewer: | Right, so anything – you don't have to feel that to have sex with somebody? |
| Paul: | Not really, no. |

For many of the young women in The Respect Study, one of the legitimating reasons to have sex was to be in love. If you loved him, and you thought he might be 'the one' for you, then it could be all right to embark on a sexual relationship. If it was a casual relationship, such as a one-night stand, or sex done just for the pleasure of the moment, this was, for most young women, not quite right. Donna and Sonia (quoted above), both stressed the importance of love in any sexual relationship, and differentiated between sex and making love, as did Lola.

> Sex is just sex, but making love is love, in'it? It's two different things –
> to me it's two different things.
> *Lola, aged 14*

Love and romance are an acceptable part of a young woman's vocabulary but for young men it can be more complicated. While it is very possible for them to feel emotion, fall in love, and respect women, they may not feel able to publicly admit this to friends (apart, perhaps, from a close male confidante). Young men use humour and teasing as a way of policing their own behaviour. They are subject to male peer pressure and may be contending with several contradictions in how they can or wish to be seen. At one level, they want to have sex and be seen as a stud by their group of mates, and if this means they have to declare love to a young woman (whether or not they mean it), so be it. But at another level, showing or declaring love is also risky for their image, and could result in them being teased for being soft. This was exemplified by a small group of Northern Irish young men who were discussing these kinds of issues shortly before St Valentine's Day. Whether or not they had girlfriends, or fancied anyone, they felt it was not done for them to show any overt romanticism. But they also acknowledged that it was partly a function of their age in feeling vulnerable to being made fun of by their peers, and they recognised that adults can be more romantic because they have 'learned not to care'. Young women do not have such a conflict; they can be romantic and yet not be seen as 'soppy'. Therefore using and being comfortable with such a romantic discourse is something that is gendered, it is partly a function of age and experience and, to some extent, has to be learned.

The traditional distinctions made between men's and women's reasons for being initially attracted to the opposite sex still appeared to hold: women go more for personality and generally positive feelings about a man, while men are more focused on physical appearance. The group of 15- to 16-year-old young people in Northern Ireland quoted below, endorsed this view and reflected what appears to be young men's greater desire for sex, and women's for emotional attachment.

Interviewer:	Do you think you should love somebody – it makes it important?
Adele:	You must have to feel something.
Simon:	Horny.
Adele:	Everybody must feel something towards them in order to be attracted.
Glen:	Good body.

While 'good' sex for young women can include sex based on love, for young men at this age, what is 'good' for them is perhaps more based on their performance, rather than their feelings. Sex and love are obviously not exclusive, but they certainly do not always come together. In a group where most were critical of sex without love, one young woman suggested that the one could lead to the other: 'You would have sex when you were in love but then it might start off as sex and then you might be making love in the end, mightn't you?'

One of the attractions of love as a way of legitimising sex is that it is associated with the status of adulthood and with maturity. The extent to which it is realistic for young people to be able to handle the powerful emotions involved and the potential for others to exploit such emotions is commented on by Aideen, who considered that at this stage in their lives young people do not really know what love is.

> 'Cause they might be only, what, fifteen and you love someone then? Know what I'd say to him 'No chance' ... And some people don't know what love is when they're our age too.
> *Aideen, aged 14*

Play: Sex as legitimised by pleasure

The media is very sexualised, and usually portrays sex as something almost irresistible and ultimately very pleasurable. Yet in real life it was harder for young people to legitimate having sex simply for pleasure, without the fear that this might label them as immoral. This was the contradiction in endorsing a set of sexual values around fun and pleasure. It is another gendered view, that young men find it easier to support than young women. As Sue Lees showed in her research, young women are constantly monitoring whether they might be labelled as 'slags' if they seem too keen on sex or go with 'too many' men, while young men get away with being a 'stud', or simply 'horny' (Lees 1986, 1993). Apart from gender, in some locations where religious values were strong, such as Northern Ireland, there was more moral disapproval of having sex simply for pleasure. For example, 14- and 15-year-olds Aideen and Roma, were somewhat shocked at the idea that some people do have sex for enjoyment.

Aideen:	... but I think that just some people enjoy it. [giggles] I'm being serious, like some people do.
Roma:	Nah, but still, it's not right. You don't go round having sex with everyone just 'cause you like it!
Aideen:	It's like a hobby; it's just like somebody doing netball –

In another group of Irish young people, 15-year-old Cheryl was one of several who disagreed that love was necessary to have sex, but thought that people needed at least to have some positive feelings about the person they had sex with.

'cos sex is something like ... I dunno, it's just sort of ... you don't have to LOVE someone ... Well it would need to be someone that you LIKED anyway ... someone that you like and someone that you sort of felt something about them.

Cheryl

While many young women wish to make love the necessary condition for sex, some young men make the distinction between the sort of women they would have sex with, and those who they would fall in love with and possibly marry. This could happen in any culture, but in our study was most apparent among young people from backgrounds where the religion or culture does not condone women having sex outside marriage, so the ideal is to marry a virgin. Men, however, do not want to limit their own sexual experience before marriage, so may look to find a woman who is willing to have sex with them but who they are likely to reject as marriage material. This is an age-old double standard which leaves the woman concerned in a very weak position; and feeling even more undermined if she only lost her virginity in the belief that the man would stay with her permanently or, preferably, marry her.

Kerby, aged 16, also described a double standard. He strongly asserted that girls have the same sexual desires as young men, nevertheless, he equally strongly contended that it was okay for boys to sleep with girls, but it was clear that he would still denigrate any girl who sleeps with several people, wears a certain style of clothes, or who in some way he viewed as 'slack'.

> Boys think, well, if this girl's slack with four or seven boys she's nasty, but I think boys and girls are the same. They've both got the same emotions. Both get the same feelings – if they wanna do it, they gotta do it. I'm not saying so they're not nasty for that, but some, certain girls, the way they do it though. The way they present themselves. They are slack women. All them short, short skirts. There's no need for them short skirts ... I always put them in categories. Easy or not easy. When a girl's easy I have no respect for them at all. Treat them differently from a girl that ain't. I talk to them different ... Once a girl's just given away, giving herself to you, take it, I know all boys'll take it.
>
> *Kerby*

This kind of double standard can make having sex for pleasure a risky business for young women. If they have 'too many' sexual relationships it can affect how they are viewed by their male peers (such as we saw with Kerby), and sometimes how their female peers view them too. They consequently gain 'a reputation', as discussed in the next section. What may feel good to experience, may be seen through the moral lens as 'bad'.

Sex as legitimised by pleasure was something seen as much more the prerogative of young men, because they did not have to worry about pregnancy.

> Interviewer: You think boys do it for enjoyment?
> Orla: Aye, it's all they ever talk about.
> Interviewer: So why is it enjoyable for boys and not for girls?
> Ella: Because boys know they're not going to get pregnant.
>
> *16-year-olds in Northern Ireland*

Alcohol and sex make a familiar combination at any age, and getting drunk is often part of a pleasurable night out for both sexes. It is a particular 'risky' situation – recognised by both young men and women – that invokes several competing values regimes of pleasure, romance, pressure and safety. And it can lead to people doing things they may later regret, like having sex. For some of the young people in The Respect Study, it seemed that having too much to drink was quite a common explanation for a young person having sex (and this is true for older people too) but it is not a legitimising reason. It is accepted that sex 'under the influence' can and does happen, but this is still classified under 'bad sex'. It often means just a one-off event, which is not morally justified, may well not involve any pleasure for the young woman, and may mean both parties have problems in remembering exactly what happened. They thought that girls get bolder and a bit reckless after drinking, and may use this, or getting stoned on drugs, as a subsequent 'excuse' for having had sex.

> We like drinking ourselves and everything so we've got the excuse – 'oh, I was wrecked out me face, I was this, I was that' – but they all get stoned and everything as well so they use that as an excuse.
> *Kerry, aged 14*

Some 14- to 15-year-old young women also observed that boys became sexually bolder after they had been drinking, and suggested that this generally starts happening when they reach the age of about 14 years old.

Kerry:	As soon as they all start drinking, that's it – they're right up there and then they think they can do anything.
Rosie:	Do anything, yeah.
Kerry:	And then they drink and deny the fact that they've done anything.
Rosie:	They can just say 'Oh it wasn't my fault, I was pissed.'

Drink may provide the 'Dutch courage' to have sex at all, and may be a fairly common prelude for unintentional sex for people of any age, but is often an occurrence that is looked back on with some regret, especially by young women, and particularly if it constituted their first experience of sex. For them, this initial sexual encounter may not involve pleasure at all (Holland and others 1998), and some Northern Irish young women were not anticipating pleasure whenever it happened, like 16-year-old Ella and Maureen.

Interviewer:	Do you expect sex to be something that's nice or something that's horrible?
Ella:	No. Horrible.
Maureen:	It's something I don't want to think about, as long as I can. [giggles]

Security: Sex as legitimised by commitment

> I think, yeah, Christianity – no sex before marriage. I'm sure there's so many people who are real faithful to Christianity but they do have sex before they've been married. I think that's too restricted really.
> *Elliott, aged 13*

Lorraine:	I think (religion is) good in a way – because it stops all teenage pregnancy and –
Yasmin:	That's if you respect your religion.

14- to 15-year-olds

Moral and religious views differ from culture to culture, and although there was not a great ethnic diversity in the young people comprising The Respect Study, there were strong religious beliefs underlying those from the Catholic and Protestant communities in Northern Ireland, as well as those from other cultures such as South Asian, East Asian and African-Caribbean. Relevant for many of these beliefs is the negative significance of having 'sex outside marriage'. Marriage implies a commitment beyond a belief in 'love', a belief or a commitment to cultural customs or expectations.

'Sex outside marriage' was one of the items that the young people had to judge in the questionnaire, and it produced a mixed and similar response from both sexes. Young men's and women's responses tended to be polarised, with 44 per cent saying that this was rarely or never wrong, and 34 per cent asserting that it was always or usually wrong. These responses were clearly affected by other factors, such as religious or ethnic backgrounds and beliefs, and hence also location. For example, those in Northern Ireland, especially young women, were more in favour of sex within marriage, and marriage in general, than many others in different parts of England (Sharpe 2001). But some young women in Northern Ireland held mixed views on keeping sex within marriage, and while some agree with marriage, others, such as 16-year-old Orla, thought that this was unrealistic and a husband would leave you anyway, as it is so easy to get a divorce.

Interviewer:	Do you think sex should only be within marriage?
Ella:	Aye.
Orla:	Not really because if the girl going to have a baby she's left to bring it up herself. He could just clear off anyway. I wouldn't. So, if you're married you can easily get a divorce.

As we have seen, some young people tend to morally disapprove of having sex simply for pleasure. It was 15-year-old Roma, from Northern Ireland (quoted earlier), who considered that you should not treat sex in the same way as you might a hobby like netball! But for others, the prohibition on sex was more than a sense of social morality; it was something formed by the moral codes of their family's religion. Fourteen-year-old Yasmin, for example, was Turkish, her family was Muslim, and although they did not follow a very strict religious practice, she was expected to have a marriage approved by her parents and their religion, if not actually arranged. She suggested that some religions, such as her own, pronounce that you cannot have sex until you are married and, despite having had a number of secret boyfriends herself, she believed that this restriction might be a good thing and could help to prevent unwanted pregnancy. Her relationships had not been sexual and she was determined to keep it that way until she got married.

Lola:	Say if you went home and your mum found out you was pregnant what would happen to you?
Yasmin:	She'd beat me (laughs) ... I wouldn't be allowed to have the baby. I don't know – I don't know, I've never had to do that, you know? – I can tell her anything but if I went home and told her I was pregnant I don't know what – it's best to do
Interviewer:	Do you worry about things like getting pregnant?
Yasmin:	No, 'cos I wouldn't do it yet –

Yasmin's attitude and constancy in saying 'No' to sex means that she will be seen more favourably as a potential marriage partner by young men from her culture. Where sex before marriage is viewed with disapproval (particularly for women), this fuels young men's division of women into those they would have sex with (but not marry) and those who they would marry. Although there are more love marriages nowadays in such cultures living in Britain, and even some cohabitation, the strict moral codes are still generally upheld in most families and the community. This was also the case in some Catholic families in Northern Ireland.

Sex was also seen as legitimate if located within a long-term relationship. The extent to which such commitment was dependent on marriage (or an intention to marry) varied among the sample. In Northern Ireland, strictures against premarital sex are eroding and the etiquette of sexual experimentation was the site of some interest. As Roma commented, if a couple is 'looking towards marriage', then sex would be expected. But as she then went on to acknowledge that even if a long term couple were not contemplating marriage, some sexual activity is going to be on the cards simply because of the time scale of the relationship.

If you don't want to get married you're going to have to do something if you've been going with him for ages and ages.
Roma

Northern Irish Orla considered that any young woman should know what her prospective husband is like. She thought that men change when you move in with them and argued for living with someone before you marry.

> Aye. I think that it's far better if you live with somebody but it's [worse] if you go with somebody for ages and then you're going to get married and then they always change when you move in with them ... you have to know what they're like and what their habits are.
>
> *Orla, aged 16*

What is most striking about the young people's responses cited here is the value that they attribute to security within a sexual relationship. Marriage here appears to be valued primarily because it protects the female party from a negative sexual reputation and provides some security in the event of pregnancy. Significantly, these young people do not talk in terms of sin, or the sanctity of marriage. Rather, they value the institution of marriage for the commitment it represents, even though some question the reliability of the security it offers.

Equity: Sex as legitimised by consent

Whether or not boys and young men are keener on having sex, and girls and young women are generally keener on love and romance, it is certainly the case that sex seems to occupy more of young men's conversation than it does young women's. This can produce a kind of pressuring from young men to young women that can distort any consequent mutual consent for sex. Thus the gendering of these kinds of views placed young women in the position of fearing or experiencing possible sexual exploitation by men, while many young men simply saw sex and love as different and both were acceptable. For example, 15-year-old Abbey was concerned that she would only want to have sex 'if you know that person's going to respect you and not just use you'. She was suspicious of men's motives in their declarations of love, and suggested: 'They may say they love you just to have sex with you.' These suspicions were confirmed by some 16-year-old young people.

> Interviewer: Would it be all right to pretend – to tell somebody you loved them and have sex with them?
>
> Glen: Happens every day.
>
> Adele: That's what fellas do.
>
> Robert: It happens all the time.

It is these kinds of statements and knowledge that fuel young women's general agreement that all that young men want is sex. A young woman may be mistaken or misled in the belief that her young man really wants sex because he loves her. In a group of 14- to 15-year-olds, Lola and Lorraine suggested that the test for love is if the boy stays with you after he's asked for sex and you have refused him.

Lola:	When they want to have sex with you – then you know when they love you, you tell them no and they – then you know they love you.
Interviewer:	What – if they accept that you don't want it?
Lorraine:	Yea, but if you wanted to have sex and you feel it's the right moment the way to test them is to say 'No' and see how they react – if they say 'oh, that's all right', then you say, all right then, let's have sex (laughs) – that's if you're ready for it though.

Sometimes consenting to sex turns out to be a mistake and this can be the result of pressure coming from other young people. Peer pressure in some form emerged as an important aspect of early sexual activity. When discussing sexual pressure in the focus groups, the young people seemed to take this as meaning two forms: a physical or verbal pressure between two individuals (usually male pressurising female) to have sex, which may even lead to rape; or a general pressure from peers on an individual to lose their virginity (to 'do it'). Part of the attraction of sex is it being a step on the road to adult status, the markers of which, as we have discussed, have become increasingly dispersed over the teenage years. For young men, this was expressed more in terms of the expectations from their male friends to have done something sexual, and to talk (or boast) about their own sexual performance (Holland and others 1993, 1998). In the questionnaire, the judgement by the young people about whether pressurising someone to have sex was wrong showed that the majority, not surprisingly, condemned this activity. Of the young people, 71 per cent considered it to be 'always wrong', and only a total of 14 per cent thought that it was 'sometimes', 'rarely' or 'never' wrong. Amidst this general consensus, gender was again in evidence, with the young women being significantly more disapproving than the young men (81 per cent: 62 per cent thought it was 'always wrong'; and 3 per cent: 10 per cent that it was 'rarely/never wrong').

A group of 13- to 14-year-old young men from London, and Paul from the North of England, also discussed this issue and acknowledged the peer pressures involved.

Lee:	I think you should do it when you're ready to do it –
Elliot:	Absolutely, that's true –
Gus:	– yea, when you're ready.
Taylor:	– when you think you're ready – no-one should force you to do it –
Gus:	Yea, there's a lot of peer pressure – Yea, some people – some friends will tend to go 'you gotta do it man'.
Elliot:	You're a VIRGIN!

13- to 14-year-olds in London

Lots of people just do it for attention. Like just going round sleeping with everyone. Everyone just thinks it's big round here and just agree with it and so everyone just does it. Boys and girls – they both say it. I'm not saying they expect it but round here most people think it's right.
Paul, aged 16

Young women are susceptible to both kinds of pressure, not only from their boyfriends wanting sex, but some also experience pressures from some of their female peers to lose their virginity, who may deride them if they do not.

Sonia:	The under-age people only do it because you're getting called – like you're boring and everything so they're getting ...
Tanya:	Pressure.
Sonia:	Yea, and they just go and do it.
Tanya:	Yea they do it to fit in with their friends and that.

14- to 15-year-olds from the North of England

As part of the continuing expectations on men to be the sexual initiators, there is an expectation that women will be expected to put up some level of resistance, especially if they think this lack of acquiescence confirms them as not being 'easy'. This may become part of a ritual in sexual negotiations. But gender relations have been gradually changing over the years, and there was some acknowledgement that girls may not be prepared to put up with such pressure, as 16-year-old Lorna observed.

Girls are getting a lot more, erm, most girls, ninety-nine per cent of them, getting a lot more – 'I don't want to, I'm not going to. Enough' I've been pressured, not pressured, but put in that situation ... twice. I just said 'I don't want to,' so he said, 'That's fine.' Boys don't pressure girls anymore.

> It's not worth it, they get too much hassle. Don't know why they bother, to
> be quite honest.
> *Lorna*

In one group of 14- to 15-year-olds, Estelle suggested that 'sometimes it might be the
other way round because sometimes boys are a bit shy'. Nevertheless, the general
belief still seemed to rest on the assumption that young men take the initiative, and
hence the possibility that the pressure is on young women. This was enhanced by the
cliché, denied by most women, but endorsed by many men that 'If a girl says "No"
she doesn't really mean it.' This was one of the contentious statements discussed in
several of the focus groups and this gender distinction was quite clear, as Estelle and
Kerby illustrated.

> I just think that when a girl's not ready she'll say that she's not ready, she
> won't actually say she's not ready and mean that she's ready.
> *Estelle, aged 14*

> (Girls) need sex as much as we do. That's the way I see it. Like girls going
> like – like you get the proper tight girls, like 'oh no, I don't wanna have
> sex', but you know they want it as well, because they got the same feelings
> that you got. They want it as well, so what they going all stupid for?
> *Kerby, aged 16*

But not all young men ascribed to this view.

> If you are a proper like person, well, not like proper person, but if you like
> understand what she's saying then you will respect her wishes that she's not
> sure so you just have to wait till she is sure.
> *Nam, aged 15*

Despite this assertion, Nam participated in a male group discussion of this statement
in which the group generally endorsed the belief that a young woman might not
necessarily mean what she says.

Kofi:	Some people they like to tease, you know – some people they say, like *[in a put-on voice]* 'No, I don't want it'.
Raja:	Yea, like if they say it like that they do mean it.
Kofi:	If they she says *[in another put-on voice]* 'NO, I don't want it' –
Raja:	– and then you run –
Kofi:	– you'd know – If she said 'No', then she means it.
Nam:	She'd say 'No, later', and I'd say 'When?'

Kofi:	But some people say it in other ways, and they don't hear that. Some people like see it in other ways – they go saying 'No', but then they're only joking – and then they rape them in the end.
Clive:	Yea – if she says it in a funny way.
Kofi:	Then you're not sure. But if she says no way anytime, that's it – I put my trousers back on and go home.
Interviewer:	So, what's saying 'No' in a funny way?
Clive:	'NOOoooo'

14- to 15-year-olds

Although young women are not meant, in young men's eyes, to 'want it', young men can be clearly confused by apparent 'sexual signals' being sent by young women in the way they dress.

Kofi:	It doesn't matter what a girl is wearing, 'cos she could be wearing something that is so revealing, but still say 'No', and that. Because she is wearing that, you could think that she is only joking, but if she says 'No' then she says 'No', and you don't. There ain't nothing more to think about.
Raja:	To me it does because – if she wears stuff like that she wants guys to look at her.
Kofi:	But that's just looking in'it, it's not doing.
Raja:	To me it is, anyway.

Many young people are aware of, or have actually experienced, sexual pressures. This did not make them any easier to resist, especially if the pressure was coming from someone they thought might be the 'right one' for them. In terms of young people's morality, it is not 'good' sex, but it represents a traditional gender distinction whereby young men still think that the sexual initiative lies in their hands and, for a variety of reasons, they will use it. Although sex may be legitimised in their view by mutual consent, the gendered process of sexual negotiation means that sexual pressure may be inadvertently (as well as deliberately) exerted.

Legality: Sex as legitimised by the law

| Interviewer: | Why do you think the law is there? |
| Seamus: | To try and stop people from doing it. |

Kirsty:	To protect people.
Interviewer:	To protect people – in what way?
Kirsty:	From getting pregnant when they're under age. And then there's other things like AIDS and all that there.
Rosa:	It gives them a better education – the pupils and all.
Pauline:	And time to live their life too.

13- to 14-year-olds

For most young people the 'right time' for sex is not related to the law on sexual age of consent.[4] Yet, regardless of the existence of a legal age limit, the young people in The Respect Study had no hesitation in making moral judgements on having sex at an early age. In the questionnaire, they were asked to judge whether they thought 'Sexual intercourse under the age of 16' was wrong. Half of them considered this to be 'always/usually wrong', and proportionally more of the young women (59 per cent) than the young men (44 per cent) took this view. There was, however, a significant group of them who thought that under-age sex was 'rarely' or 'never wrong' (25 per cent), and this comprised 32 per cent of the young men and 18 per cent of the young women. It is likely that the gender difference here was related both to young men's generally greater involvement in sex or at least the idea of sex (and certainly this was assumed by both sexes), and also young women's fears and concerns about possible pregnancy.

Under-age sex emerged as a salient dilemma in The Respect Study. The young people were asked in the questionnaire to describe a dilemma typical for their age. This was defined for them as 'a situation in which it is difficult to decide what is the right thing to do'. Two-thirds of them gave at least one dilemma, and many raised several. Overall, the most common themes reported in young people's dilemmas were drugs, under-age sex (19 per cent), smoking and alcohol. Social or peer pressure seems to underpin many of their dilemmas, including this one. Under-age sex seems to become an increasing concern with increasing age, as seen in the responses of the 11-year-olds through to the 16-year-olds. This was particularly the case amongst young women. Overall, 23 per cent of young women and 14 per cent of young men were concerned with

---

4 This age is 16 years in England for heterosexual young people, but 17 years in Northern Ireland, which was the home of a significant number of the young people in this study. For gay men, the age of consent is now 16, in line with the law on heterosexual sex. The average age of first sex in the United Kingdom is around 17, but a significant number of young people experience sexual intercourse under the legal age of consent of 16. The age at which young people first have sex in Britain has been steadily falling, and a significant minority will have sexual intercourse before they are legally entitled to do so (Johnson and others 1993; Wellings, 2001).

under-age sex in their cited dilemmas. In certain urban locations, for example North Park school, a deprived Northern England school, under-age sex (and pregnancy) were the most frequently mentioned dilemmas. Once more this was enhanced for young women (31 per cent: 15 per cent). In South Park, an inner city school in the South of England, under-age sex was also the most cited dilemma but here it was of equal concern to both sexes. Both sites were characterised by being predominantly working class, in whose culture early sexual experience and pregnancy have been nothing unusual and may be accepted, if not desired.

The law on sexual offences was introduced in the Criminal Law Amendment Act 1885, in order to protect young women from predatory men, by prohibiting men having intercourse with a woman aged under 16. It has recently been reformed to remove the gender bias within existing formulations of consent (although the law of consent itself is not changing). In their group discussions around the age of consent law, the young people illustrated the gap between law and policy, and everyday life. The proposal contained in the focus group statement that: 'The age of consent for heterosexual sex should be lowered from 16 to 14', generally caused some confusion.

Young people took different approaches to this law and whether they felt it should be changed or not. Miles, aged 13, from a well-off area in the Home Counties, was not alone in his assumption that when young people reach the legal age for sex, they would instantly go out and have it.

> I think it's sort of like a bit stupid at the moment because like 16 is like – you get all these 16-year-olds O.K., on their sixteenth birthday, who like, have sex and then in the next nine months, before they're 17, they have a baby and then they haven't even finished school yet, they'd just be like in the lower sixth, and then they've sort of got this baby on their hands and they haven't even like, could not even have a first boyfriend or a husband, like, they'd have to either quit school or put it up for adoption which is ... sort of like immature.
> *Miles*

Several others similarly talked as though young people would simply start having sex as soon as they hit the legal age of 16. For this reason they disagreed with lowering it to the age of 14.

> Some people, they're sixteen, when they turn sixteen, well, they just go out and sleep with anybody, they shouldn't do that. You shouldn't sleep with

somebody who you're with for a while 'cos you don't know if they've got AIDS or anything.

Jodie, aged 13

Therefore changing the legal age of consent was not seen as a good idea because young people would go and have sex merely because they were legally eligible to do so and it would thus lead to more teenage pregnancies. This is perhaps underestimating the sensibility of their own peers, although it is reasonable to suppose that the younger the people start having sex, the less likely it will be that they have the maturity to enjoy and take responsibility for sex.

With this risk in mind, some saw the law as a kind of 'protection' against pregnancy, because they saw 14 as far too young to have a baby.

Francis:	The law could be nine – it's not going to change things.
Jacqueline:	It is something to hide behind if they wanted, they've got the excuse, haven't they.
Keith:	But if you're ready you're ready, aren't you?
Jacqueline:	It's a protective for them.

15-year-olds

Evelyn, from London, also thought lowering the age of consent would result in younger people having babies, but took her disapproval a step further in pointing out the unlikelihood of there being a father around.

'Cos if you're older you're more likely to stay with the person you had sex with and to look after the baby with you, but the young guy they just like leave you – they don't really want to be tied down.

Evelyn, aged 14

Another aspect was raised by some of the young people in the study who considered that reducing the age of consent might further increase the pressure on girls to have sex. Thirteen-year-old Sarah was one of these.

Some people – if it was lowered to fourteen then like girls – 'cos like if it was like lowered to fourteen then next year I could have it and it's just stupid – because everybody will be like that, oh, I'm fourteen now I can go and have sex with anybody I want to ... You might not want it yet and some boy might say, oh, you're fourteen now, you can have sex and everything.

Sarah

The age of consent law brings in complex social and personal issues, as well as legal ones.

| Kay: | It's like putting an age on loving – that you're not allowed to love if you're under fourteen. |
| Naomi: | 'Cos you can't control your feelings by a law, can you? |

14- to 15-year-olds

Another reason why young people thought it was quite irrelevant to change the law on consent related to the points made earlier about the 'right time' for sex. Most young people agreed that they and others did not accept the authority of the law on this, and observed that 'most people don't go by the law'. While many found themselves supporting the age of 16, and a few even suggesting that it be raised to 18, they were at pains to clarify that, for them, it was not the law in itself that made sex legitimate but a range of other more individual and personal factors. Some challenged the imposition of public rules on an area of such private intimacy, but they were not happy about dispensing with laws and rules altogether, however ambivalent they may have been about restrictions from authority. This was especially the case for the young women.

> I don't think the girls' age should be lowered to fourteen – I think that's a bit young 'cos I mean you might be physically ready but you might not be emotionally ready for what's going to happen – like you might not be able to deal with things that come afterwards.
> *Jade, aged 14*

> I think if you lower the age to fourteen they go: 'Oh, yea, that's great, you know, oh, yea, 'cos I can be like everybody – I can be like my sister ... ' and everything, but because they do it, sometimes girls feel cheap and dirty about it afterwards 'cos they just thought, 'Oh, great,' but it's not as good as they thought it would be.
> *Marion, aged 13*

A group of 14- to 15-year-olds living around a rural village were more of the opinion that there was no real need for a law at all, provided you knew all the risks.

Andrew:	As long as you know what you're doing – all the facts.
Helena:	You know the risks.
Andrew:	You can't really do anything after that.
Keith:	Should be your own choice.

In the same light, Elliott thought that adequate sex and relationships education would deal with this situation.

> I think like – I quite agree 'cos there's still a lot of responsible kids round

> here and if we have a good sex and relationships education in schools then people will know of the advantages of sex and the disadvantages, if you get what I mean, so if we're taught properly I think we could have it at fourteen – around like you could start like having sex in Year 8 or something, or Year 9 – something like that –
> *Elliott, aged 13*

There was some polarisation of views reflecting agency and lack of agency. Whereas Keith (above) for example, thought it was individual choice, for some of the young people there seemed to be a sense of fatalism or inevitability about when people like themselves had sex which made any law redundant. This implies an absence of agency, which is worrying, although they also asserted that they would know what they were doing.

> If you're going to do it you're going to do it – government or your parents can't stop you really – but I think the age is okay, I mean in some countries it's as young as twelve and it's pretty ridiculous that.
> *Steven, aged 14*

> I don't think it's like really wrong to do it at fourteen – we're going to do it anyway.
> *Joe, aged 13*

If these young people found the idea of trying to regulate the time people had sex as impossible, and endorsed the notion that they would inevitably have sex when they chose, and, with a bit of luck, at the 'right time', it is no wonder that they took a dim view of enforcing the age of consent laws.

> You can't really say it's illegal because they can't go round everywhere getting all people who've done it under sixteen – and putting them in prison or anything.
> *Carla, aged 14*

Some suggested that parents may have more legitimate authority than the law, but the young people's responses suggested that sexual agency was a very personal and private realm in which they did not expect the state or parents to be in a position to intervene in their own decisions.

> No one is gonna force me – it's up to me – nobody can force me what to do – tell me what to do.
> *Gus, aged 13*

This obviously makes the age of consent a difficult law to implement, as Keith observed.

> It's sort of like in law, but it's sort of not there, is it? It's not sort of like a crime or drugs or whatever.
> *Keith, aged 15*

The young people also pointed to the apparent discrepancies and unfairness of the law in that, for example, a 17-year-old young woman could have sex with a 14-year-old boy and not be potentially prosecuted for it. But despite not wanting such legal intervention, the young people did not argue for the abolition of the age of consent in fact, if anything, some were more in favour of raising it from 16 to 18. This was often in the context of discussing the issue of sexual abuse of children by adults.

But while some young women felt they would be made vulnerable through lowering the age of consent, some young men suggested that sex could make them vulnerable too, whether it involved pressure or not, if it turned into an accusation of rape. They were concerned that a young woman could consent to sex and then think better of it and declare that she had been forced to have sex, that is, she had been raped. One group of 12- to 13-year-old boys from the rural school talked about this, and discussed the possibility of a girl changing her mind after the event to say that she was raped, especially if she had got pregnant as a consequence.

Joe:	It's up to the girl though, in' it? 'Cos if you have sex and they know it now, it's like rape or something.
Guy:	Not if they say that they want it.
Paul:	No, 'cos – then they get pregnant – they could say they didn't want it.
Guy:	Yea, I know.
Liam:	They can get money for it, can't they?
Joe:	Yea, and you get arrested for it.

The various criteria for sexual readiness can be understood as the factors that make a sexual relationship personally and socially legitimate. Trust and freedom from pressure are crucial, as are the maintenance of self-respect and a respectable sexual reputation. At the heart of the current law on the heterosexual age of consent are very strong messages about gender and sexual agency, which stand in contradiction to the way in which many young people would like to think about themselves. There is a clear tension here between legal and lay notions of consent, the former speaking in terms of protection, and the latter in terms of rights. What was clear from their discussions was that, although they expressed the desire to be respected and trusted, they also recognised the importance of publicly negotiated rules in the form of the law. And, while they may ignore these rules, they also engage with them in the creation of their sexual cultures. It appears that for young people, it is less important that sex is legal or protected than for it to be 'timely', a delicate state of social and interpersonal acceptability.

> I don't think it makes a difference because if they feel ready then they're going to do it. It's not like anyone can keep watch over them and say – they can't really stop it ...
> *Heather, aged 14*

Safety: Sex as legitimised by its consequences

> But I shouldn't think that anyone who's actually like young and has a child actually planned to have the child – if you plan it then you must be able to support it, if you can't support it then you obviously haven't planned it.
> *Richard, aged 16*

One of the ways in which sex was moralised by young people was in relation to its consequences. Thus it was not so much the sexual experience itself that was important (be that in terms of pleasure or love) but the consequences of that experience that classified it as 'good' or 'bad' sex. Thus one way in which sex takes on a moral meaning for young people is within a values regime of 'safety': they may risk their reputation, they may contract a sexually transmitted infection (STI), or they may become pregnant and have to face the subsequent decision to keep the child or have an abortion. Of these risks, young men only really face the possibility of an STI, as their reputation is usually left unharmed by a sexual encounter, and pregnancy and abortion may involve their minds, but not their bodies. Here the young people in The Respect Study discuss these issues: sexual reputation and pregnancy.

Reputation

Sonia:	Most people haven't – we hang around in a big group and there's only one girl in our group who hasn't been – you know, kissed anyone and she always gets called but we don't call her 'cos we know what it's like and –
Interviewer:	And what would you get called – what name would you get?

| Sonia: | Frigid. Or just – they don't usually say that any more, they just say – |
| Donna: | You've not even been with anybody. |

14- to 15-year-old young women from the North of England

The first consequence of a young person having a sexual relationship is the possibility of gaining some kind of reputation. For a young man, this is generally a good thing – he's a stud, he has 'had a result', and he may waste no time in informing his male peers, perhaps embroidering the tale on the way. This was clearly the case in the research carried out in the early 1990s, when in a project on sexual negotiation (Holland and others 1998), young men recounted performance stories to their friends, and it was almost necessary for them to have had, or at least to say that they have had, some kind of sexual experience with a woman. For a young woman, the prospect of getting a reputation is a daunting one (Lees 1986, 1993; Holland and others 1998). It generally has negative connotations, whether or not she has had any sex at all. If she has sex, she is in danger of being called a slag, or easy, or a number of other labels. If she refuses to have sex, she may get a reputation as frigid or tight, although there is some hope that she may gain respect for saying 'No' to sex. In the context of our concepts of 'good' and 'bad' sex, sex that endangers a young woman's reputation can be viewed as 'bad sex' although she may not realise this until afterwards.

Reputation and 'calling' were mentioned frequently by the young people in The Respect Study, within the various topics under discussion. It came up for Jade, for example, in the context of possibly lowering the age of consent for sex to 14.

> Like just say you was to have sex at like fourteen and then like the guy would – 'cos guys are just like that – they might not talk to you the next day and they like go around and tell all their friends and everything and you're really regretting it – you would have wished that you'd have waited until you were sixteen or something like that then you'd be able to deal with it.
>
> *Jade, aged 14*

Whether 16 is the magic age for dealing with sex is questionable, but clearly young women, particularly within a school group culture, may be very vulnerable to such a labelling process. Other groups also talked about reputation and the double standard that this involved.

> There's such a difference like. Because if WE sleep around we'll be called slags, – if THEY sleep about they get called macho, and one of the lads.
>
> *Cheryl, aged 15*

For Charlotte, there also seemed to be a fine balance about how much you went about with lads or with other girls. Too much time with lads and you're a slag; too much time with girls and you're a lesbian.

> And if you talk to the lads and you're seen with the lads – 'Oh, you are a tart, you are a slut,' but if you're seen with a lot of girls then, like, other people, when they never see you with, like hanging around with lads, say 'Oh you're a lesbian, you're this, you're that.'
> *Charlotte, aged 14*

It is a 'no-win' situation for young women, since they may be called a 'slag', or get some sort of reputation, whatever course of action they take. This may then gain them a sexual reputation that is erroneous, but sticks nevertheless. Sandra, who was at school in a deprived urban area in the North of England, described the pressures on girls and young women who get fancied by the young men of the moment, whether it is the current 'nice' lad or the 'cock of the year', and the consequences.

> If the dead nice lad of the year fancies you, that's good, because then other lads start fancying you ... it's good for the girls, but they expect things off yer – to go further with them and all that ... if it's like the cock of the year, or the nicest lad of the year, they ask yer, and they're thingy, it's hard to say 'No' to them because they'll go telling their mates that you've said 'No.' And then they'll tell their mates and it will get round the school that you just said 'No' to the lad, the nice lad. It is a good thing to do, but it's hard to say 'No' to them ... but some people admire it because you just – like even the quiet ones, they used to think, God, if she can say 'NO', we can ...
> *Sandra, aged 13*

Kerby presented his version of the double standard that can operate when he described his view of, and behaviour towards, girls he respected, and those he considered 'slack'.

> When girls are slack, they ain't got no, they don't get no respect, none at all ... you know, people start hassling: 'Oh come on, come on, come in the bedroom and let's do it' – and if they say, 'Oh, you're rubbish or whatnot,' in there, you've got respect for them because you know that if it was your sister or something you would hope she'd do the same thing. So you got to respect them for them not lowering theirself, or being slack. So girls get respect as well, I got a lotta respect for girls. Slack girls, I ain't got none for those ... but I don't really call girls slack, unless I talk to them first. Because

> unless I talk to a girl, I can tell if she's slack or if she's not. But I don't
> think it's fair because they just get the same needs and wants that we do ...
> *Kerby, aged 16*

Kerby's own reputation is not at all at risk, and he demonstrates just one of the many contradictions that surround sex for young people. He thought he could judge when a girl was 'slack' or not by just talking to her, and yet if she was a 'proper tight' girl and refused sex, he thought she couldn't be telling the truth because he said he believes that both sexes want sex equally. Again it seems as if young women are in a no-win situation with young men like Kerby. The young men in this research did not discuss the effect on a boy's reputation if he does not have sex, but this has been explored elsewhere. For example, one study illustrated how a young man could be seen as a 'wimp' if he did not have sex and this could invoke painful teasing from his peers (Holland and others 1993; Holland and others 1998).

Pregnancy

> Sarah: – because my mum's saying to me if you don't keep
> your head on, she says, you'll be one – so I don't want
> to have a baby dead young 'cos it would –
>
> Jodie: 'Cos if you have a baby you've got to make sure you can
> support it.
>
> *12- to 13-year-olds*

Pregnancy is an ever-present cloud on the sexual horizon. It seems bad enough for young women if they get a reputation, which can be applied whether or not any sexual activity has occurred, but if they become pregnant, this is an even more serious consequence. For younger people in particular, there seems to be a simple relationship between having sex and getting pregnant that belies the fact that they have probably had several sex and relationships education lessons informing and advising on how to prevent this through contraception and protection against STIs. Some of the focus group discussions also revealed some young people's erroneous beliefs about sex, and the possibility of reproduction. These included beliefs that young people cannot have sex until their bodies have developed properly, or that they cannot have sex until they can produce sperm, and that young women cannot get pregnant if they are having a period.

Pregnancy was a dilemma raised by 10 per cent of the young people in The Respect Study questionnaire. It was no surprise that this included more young women than young men in all age groups, and only became an issue for young men in Year 10 (aged 14–15 years). But it figured differently in the various locations, for example a greater proportion (about 15 per cent) of young men living in a deprived urban area in the North of England gave pregnancy as a dilemma compared with 3 per cent of those living in the working-class inner city location in the south of England. This may be partly explained by the more sexually restrictive ethnic backgrounds of some of the London young people. As described in the previous section, under-age sex was commonly linked with pregnancy, and was of equal concern to both sexes. For them the simple reasoning was that the younger you have sex, the greater the likelihood of becoming a young mother. The general approach was to move straight from under-age sex to how hard it would be for a young woman to care for a baby, and how this would mess up her life and opportunities.

Young people, and young women in particular, often hold the romantic belief that love can and does conquer all, even unplanned pregnancies but, while this might happen in books and films, sadly this is not always the case in real life. Fifteen-year-olds Melanie and Cheryl discussed the salutary experience of Melanie's sister.

Melanie:	She *did* love him and he loved her and he was really nice. But then when he found out she was pregnant he didn't want nothing to do with her.
Cheryl:	Well then, that there just completely defeats the purpose because you just say right, you strongly agree that they should love each other, but your sister and ...
Melanie:	But she did love him.
Cheryl:	Aye, and he loved her too and he walks away from her. So she doesn't – so if you had sex with someone that you loved and he loved you back you're still not going to know if he will stick by you or not.

Safe sex

The risk of pregnancy is of course very true, but only if the young people concerned did not practise safe sex. For most, 'safe sex' meant using contraception, more than protection against sexually transmitted infection. 'Unsafe sex' was one item on the list of activities that they had to judge in the questionnaire. Half of the young people responded that unsafe sex was 'always' or 'usually wrong' – 45 per cent of young men and 58 per cent of young women – and a quarter of them accepted that it was 'sometimes wrong'. But a surprising 19 per cent (24 per cent of the young men and 13 per cent of the young women) claimed that it was 'rarely' or 'never wrong'. The young women were more disapproving than young men of the kinds of activities that might put them at risk. And fourteen-year-old Jade was critical and somewhat unsympathetic to any young woman who did not acquaint herself with information on safe sex before she embarked on sexual activities.

> There's this girl that got pregnant – she was eleven when she got pregnant, I think – she's thirteen now and she's got a baby and she didn't even know anything about contraception but she still had sex and I think that – I mean I feel sorry for her in a way but like being lumbered with a baby at so young but she should have known better. If she didn't know about it, she shouldn't have done it, I don't think.
>
> *Jade, aged 14*

Discussion about these issues could get rather heated, and in one Northern Irish group of young women, Aideen and Hayley argued strongly about whether young women were aware of the consequences if they had sex and became pregnant.

Hayley:	Aideen, forget about being raped right and that there right. If you're going to have a baby you have to think of the consequences, you can't have a baby and then after nine months think about 'Ah I can't do this and, I can't afford to keep it on.' You should have thought about that.
Aideen:	Some people don't get a chance to think, some people don't even know they're pregnant, what about the people – do you ever read magazines or watch Rikki Lake, or watch TV – there's two wee girls –
Hayley:	Aideen, everybody knows what they're doing –
Aideen:	Hayley – NAW, THEY DON'T!
Hayley:	They do.
Aideen:	Some people have sex, and they be made pregnant and they don't know they're made pregnant. I remember reading about a girl she was that pregnant she was sitting in the bed one night and she took an urge to push and she pushed and she had a wain – now does that mean she should have thought about it first?

14- to 15-year-olds

Planning a sexual experience may be hard for some, but this may also be hindered if young people feel inhibited about buying condoms. Obtaining contraception can prove an obstacle course for some. If they want to go on the pill or get free condoms, they need to either visit the doctor, or go to a sexual health clinic. Asked in one group if they knew where the nearest Brook Clinic was, no-one could provide the answer, and it is likely that this is the case for many young people. If the pill is not an option, and condoms are chosen which also protect from STIs, it is not always a comfortable experience for young people to buy them. Jane had observed one girl trying to buy condoms in a chemist shop.

> I was in the chemist one day and there was this girl, and she was around my age – about fifteen – and she was really embarrassed, and this woman just looked at her as if to say – 'You're not old enough for (condoms).' And she just wouldn't ... she just stared her out as if to say – 'Are you seriously going to buy them?' And the wee girl was all embarrassed and she was all you know, shaking and all.
>
> *Jane, aged 15*

Getting young people to 'think about it first' is easy to say, but using contraception and practising safer sex is less easy to implement.

Conclusion

The Respect Study young people's discussion about what makes sex legitimate were characterised by inconsistency, contradiction and resistance, and moved between a range of values regimes. There were a variety of policy discourses underlying their debates, such as 'public health pragmatism' (agony aunts/uncles advice that safe sex is legitimate sex), and the 'welfarism' of concerns about early parenthood and missing out on education (as a form of social exclusion). Yet young people were also concerned to make sex morally and socially legitimate within their own terms. This is not usually within marriage, but more in a notion of agency, choice and control mediated by time, often discussed as being 'ready' for sex. This idea of readiness was flexible enough to accommodate individual and gender differences. So for one person, being ready might mean being informed and not under pressure, while for another it could mean being in a committed and stable relationship, confident and informed enough to practice safe sex. Thus, the concept of being 'ready' for sex is one that brings in physical and emotional maturity, as well as finding the appropriate person for a sexual relationship. These young people hoped or assumed that they would recognise the 'right time' and the 'right person'.

There are contradictions in the values regimes associated with 'good' and 'bad' sex.

The different aspects do not fall neatly each side of the fence. 'Good' sex may involve love and romance, and being 'safe', or in what seems to be a long-term relationship; but this can turn bad if there is pregnancy, or the relationship splits up. The jury is out on whether sex can be legitimised simply for enjoyment, and certainly not as a kind of 'hobby', as one young woman described it. With all of the values regimes described above there are significant lines of difference around gender, with young men and women being situated very differently in terms of their ability to legitimise sex. Young women are more likely to seek to legitimise sex in terms of love, and young men in terms of pleasure. While both young men and women may appear to enter the value regimes of security and equity on an equal basis, in practice these regimes are underpinned by highly gendered notions of consent and commitment. The law itself reflects highly gendered assumptions about sexual agency, and sexual safety is also recognised to fall heavily on the shoulders of young women. It is not surprising then that young men and women expressed very different views about the factors that legitimise a sexual relationship, reflecting the contrasting ways in which they are positioned in relation to notions of sexual reputation, love and romance.

Young people are able to articulate their own personal sense of sexual legitimacy. If we draw together the positive attributes from each of the values regimes described above, 'good sex' is sex that is loving, not pressured, and with no 'negative' consequences. And as with many personal issues, young people do not want to be told what to do, but wish to make up their own minds.

4. Debating sexual values

In this section we will focus on a number of distinct areas around which young people engaged in moral debate. These are:

- abortion and parenting
- sexual representation
- homosexuality.

We have chosen these areas because they provoked particularly vociferous discussion among young people, and were marked by strong differences relating to social class (abortion and parenting), gender (sexual representation and homosexuality) and ethnicity/religion (homosexuality, abortion). We have also chosen these areas because they represent arenas of sex and relationships education that cause schools and policy makers anxieties, reflecting in part their contested nature in the wider public sphere.

Abortion and parenting

We have brought together discussions of abortion with discussions of parenting here because we found that young people's views on the former bore a strong relation to their views on the latter, reflecting community and class-based cultures.

Abortion

Interviewer:	... do women have the right to have an abortion?
Cheryl:	No.
Emily:	No.
Cheryl:	Definitely not.
Sadie:	I think it's their own decision, but I think if it was me I wouldn't.

| Michelle: | I couldn't go through with it. |
| Cheryl: | I think it's really wrong because it's like murder. People now go into jail for murder – that there's just the same. |

14- to 15-year-olds in Northern Ireland

Interviewer:	So does anyone think abortion is right?
Anthony:	Yea.
Candace:	Oh, here, we go. There would be one, wouldn't there?
Anthony:	No, it's true though, if you're too young you can't look after the baby, can you? Got to finish your education first and then you're responsible enough –
Jasper:	You should stop it early then or wear the protection.

15- to 16-year-olds in London

When a young woman finds that she is pregnant, unless it is late in the pregnancy, one option is to have an abortion. This was a subject about which there were diverse views, and often strong and emotional responses. This was the case in both the questionnaire responses, and in the group discussions. Responses varied by age and by location.

There were two references to abortion in The Respect Study questionnaire. The first was where young people were asked for their responses to (or 'judgements' on) a variety of activities and behaviour. Their response to 'abortion' here tended to be somewhat polarised, but more were condemnatory than approving. Only 14 per cent of the young people in the study said that abortion was 'never wrong' or 'rarely wrong' (about 7 per cent for each). A quarter said that it was 'sometimes wrong', and half said it was 'usually wrong' or 'always wrong' (13 per cent 'usually wrong', and 37 per cent 'always wrong'). These proportions were similar for both sexes. The young people's views were significantly influenced by religion, with those professing to belong to a religion tending to assert that abortion was wrong (62 per cent), compared to 47 per cent of those with no religion. It was no surprise that most of the Catholic young people (71 per cent) were against abortion, and a majority of these lived in Northern Ireland. Although over a third of all those young people against abortion were Catholic, young Protestants from Northern Ireland were also disapproving. Apart from those without a defined religion, it was only those who said they were Christians and Muslims (although numbers were very small in the latter case), who had a majority in favour of abortion. Approval of abortion tended to vary according to self-defined religiousness, and less religious young people were predictably more approving of abortion (54 per cent), and more religious ones disapproved (78 per cent).

Age is an important factor in the development of views on abortion for many young people. Like several other sexual issues, it is with increasing age, knowledge and maturity that they recognise that situations are often much less straightforward than they originally thought. Thus, views on abortion became more liberal with increasing age, as older young people realised that the subject can be a complex dilemma. Whereas 70 per cent of those in Year 7 (11- to 12-year-olds) showed disapproval of abortion, this went down to 43 per cent for those in Year 11. Social class can also be a factor to the extent that middle-class families with high aspirations for their daughters may see teenage pregnancy as putting an end to these, and abortion as the obvious solution. In working-class families with strong educational goals, this may be equally true, but there is often a greater acceptance and normality about teenage motherhood that makes the option of an abortion less viable. Such differences in values are reflected in the differential rates of abortion in middle and working-class communities (Smith 1993).

The second occasion that the subject of abortion was raised in the questionnaire was when young people were asked: 'In your opinion, is abortion ever OK?' and 'If so, under what circumstances?' Overall, 43 per cent said that abortion is 'sometimes OK', and these included a higher proportion of young women (49 per cent) than young men (41 per cent). Exploring the circumstances in which it was deemed to be OK, these could be grouped into nine main categories, as seen in Table 4.1. The most frequently given reasons related to: the welfare of the baby, the age of the mother or parents, and a belief in the rights of the woman. The young women mainly gave reasons of age; the baby's best interests; rape; the woman's right and her health. Young men gave similar responses, but strangely more of them actually said 'the woman's right' than did the young women. More young women specified 'rape', and 'age', than did the young men. Relatively few defined the 'mother's best interests' as being an important factor, although that is clearly an important factor especially in the lives of those young women concerned about their future education or careers.

Table 4.1 The circumstances under which abortion was deemed 'okay'

	Rape	Money	Age	Health	Women's right	Baby's welfare	Mother	Other
Boys	15.1	11.2	21.7	10.5	24.3	28.9	7.2	12.2
Girls	21.2	8.7	36.1	12.8	16.0	34.5	6.0	10.9
Total	18.5	9.8	29.6	11.8	19.8	32.0	6.5	11.5

[N.B. These percentages represent the per cent of responses expressed by the boys or girls, some of whom expressed more than one response and therefore add up to more than 100 per cent.]

The issue of abortion was also discussed in the focus groups. It came up either as a statement for discussion 'It's a woman's right to choose abortion'; or in the process of discussing various other issues. These issues included: what a young woman should do if she becomes pregnant; lowering the age of sexual consent; and whether a person should only have a child if they can support it.

There were arguments in the groups about the reasons for having an abortion (which is illegal in the rest of Ireland and virtually impossibly to obtain in Northern Ireland[5]). Amongst the possible situations raised, the appropriateness of an abortion in the case of a potentially disabled child came up in one Northern Irish focus group, in a mixed but mainly Catholic working-class school. This had been fuelled by events in the TV soap opera, *Eastenders*. It is often the television soap operas that can demonstrate the real complexities and dilemmas involved in issues like abortion to the viewers, which include many young people.

> If you knew that your child was disabled, like remember Ricky and Bianca, they came across that. It had spina bifida and something on its brain and they knew that it would have hardly any quality of life. I think the mother should have the most say in it because it's a special bond.
> *Deirdre, aged 16*

However, the group were agreed about rape being another valid reason. The general thinking in this group, and in the one quoted below, was that it is more the mother's

---

5   The 1967 Abortion Act implemented in England was never extended to Northern Ireland. A motion to do so was defeated by the Assembly in 2000. Abortion is only allowed in Northern Ireland if it can be proved that pregnancy would damage the physical or mental health of the woman. The Family Planning Association in Northern Ireland estimate that every year about 2,000 women cross the sea to England from Northern Ireland to have abortions, and that in the past 20 years, 40,000 women have done so (Family Planning Association Northern Ireland Fact Sheet – Abortion. May 2003, www.healthpromotionagency.org.uk.)

right to make the decision about abortion than the father's, because it is her body that is involved.

Ruth:	The both of them should make the decision (whether to have the child) 'cos it's just as much the man's fault as it is the woman's.
Emily:	It takes two of them.
Cheryl:	It takes two to tango.
Interviewer:	What if they disagree? Does anybody have a bit more of a right than the other?
All:	The woman.
Melanie:	Because the woman's going to be carrying it for nine months and she's going to look after it more.

14- to 15-year-old young women

Although some young people supported the idea that the father should certainly be consulted, Katie, for example, questioned that if it was just the father that wanted to keep the baby, would he look after it? With the current movement of fathers who want more rights for contact with estranged children (through divorce or separation) the question of father's rights is a pertinent one.

> If there was a man – if the woman wanted to get rid of it, and the man wants to keep it, is he going to keep it on his own? Because usually the men just leave the women to deal with it, to keep the baby and have it without them.
> *Katie, aged 13*

While the Irish young people in particular had a lot to say about abortion, it was a topic also argued about by the young people in the English schools. In one mixed sex group of 15- to 16-year-olds who were mainly of African-Caribbean origin, the young women were more aware of the dilemmas and the complexities involved in having a child at a very young age, while their male peers were mainly anti-abortion, possibly seeing it as some negation of their virility.

Crystal:	If I got pregnant, yeah, and my parents chucked me out of my house, I didn't have nowhere to go, yeah, how am I going to bring up my child and look after myself. I'm still a child ... even it you're with someone probably he's just going to run off and leave me and I'm still a child. How am I going to –
Doan:	If I'm the father, I know if I got someone pregnant I'm

	not ducking off and she ain't having an abortion – I don't believe in it.
Crystal:	At the end of the day whose body is it?
Doan:	I don't care whose body –
Kerby:	From when you got it in you, it's yours – nobody else's. It's just yours 'cos that's rubbish 'cos when it comes down to payin' things, the man pays things so you can't tell him it's just yours.
Crystal:	I'd be pissed off if he's going: 'It's my baby.'
Ellen:	If the man stays it's both of yours, but if the man's gone, it's just yours mate.

Many of the young people in The Respect Study had to admit that in some cases people were simply not in the appropriate circumstances to care for and bring up a child. Abortion was particularly problematic for the young people in Northern Ireland, because of the illegality of abortion there. Thus it was not surprising that they were the most vocal in suggesting the alternative – which has been around for many years and was common in England too until the 1960s – that of adoption.

> If you had an abortion you're just killing it, but if you have adoption you're giving it a chance to live.
> *Margaret, aged 12*

Sadie:	But what's the point bringing a child into the world if you can't look after it?
Cheryl:	Adoption. There's people that are looking for children.
14- to 15-year-olds	

Thus, in certain locations, some kind of adoption was seen as more desirable than abortion, whether it was giving up the baby to an adoption agency or, as several suggested, getting their own mother to look after it as if it was her own. This latter solution has been chosen by families throughout many years of history but nowadays, even if family adoption might be a young woman's favoured choice, grandmothers may be less available or willing to take on the responsibility of substitute motherhood as they may be involved in, and enjoying, jobs or careers. Giving up a baby for adoption is not a simple thing to do, even if a young woman is keen to be rid of the pregnancy and get on with her own life (Sharpe 1987).

Having an abortion is the choice for some young people, such as those who wish to achieve educational goals, or continue to enjoy their own autonomy, and who may see it as the only alternative. But for a significant number of others, especially those with religious views or those of a very young age, it is seen as morally wrong. If the option of abortion is rejected, and the teenage pregnancy is brought to term, there is an issue of the appropriateness of becoming a mother at this age, or even at any age when you have little means of support. This brings us on to young people's views on these aspects of parenting.

Parenting

> Interviewer: So which do you think is most important to give a child, love or like financial care?
>
> All: Love!
>
> *14- to 15-year-old young women*

> I think if you know that you're not going to be able to support a child then you shouldn't get pregnant, but at the same time if it's an accident then I think you're – if you're responsible enough to go and get pregnant then you're responsible enough to look after the child – you've got to go and find a way.
>
> *Crystal, aged 16*

Parenting is a subject on which everyone may have some opinion. Although none of the young people in The Respect Study had children, they did have views on aspects of this, especially when and how it was more appropriate for someone to have a child. This was clearly touched upon when they talked about related issues of under-age sex, teenage pregnancy and abortion. It also emerged when other statements were discussed in the focus groups that suggested, for example, that people should not have a child without sufficient resources, or questioned whether children need two parents. Their attitudes to parenthood are related to their attitudes to sex, and to the values and situations of their own families, their peers, and their future expectations in terms of jobs or careers. For example, the young people located in the well-off Home Counties region reject early parenthood, mainly because of the competing values and advantages associated with getting a good education and career. In other areas, like the inner city schools in the north and south of England, this attitude was somewhat different, and there was often less assumption of, and investment in, education. Here young parenthood was more frequent and more acceptable.

One of the statements discussed was 'It is wrong to have a child unless you can support it'. This brought up a debate between those who endorsed the over-riding importance and sufficiency of love in a child's life, and those who placed more emphasis on the need for material and financial support. To some extent this was a social class issue in that it was those young people, particularly the young women, from the working-class areas who supported the view that love would provide the answer. This did not preclude material support, but they saw this as being insufficient alone. Michelle from a Northern Ireland school held this view.

> The child mightn't have, you know, money to have to be – you know to have all these nice clothes and all, but as long as the child's loved and cared about, it doesn't really matter.
> *Michelle, aged 14*

Fifteen-year-old Roma was more aware of the real impact of lack of support, and thought that if you cannot support a child then you cannot give it as much opportunity as other children.

> There's no point in bringing a child into the world unless you can support it – make its life miserable. You wouldn't be able to feed it or look after it ... Hasn't got as much care as you can. But you can't give it as much opportunity as other children – know what I mean.
> *Roma*

Roma was from a working-class background, but overall it tended to be middle-class young people in the study who stressed the need to provide the material basis for having children. All the young people in one group in a school situated in a well-off commuter belt strongly agreed that you should not have a child unless you can support it, and in most cases, their own parents had been more than able to support them, unlike many of the others participating in the research. And again, it was mainly the young women who voiced an opinion. Lorna, for example, living in a large detached house in a country village, thought that you should only have a child if you could provide for it, but was aware that not everyone was in that position.

> You should only have a child if you can give it some sort of decent life. It's not fair to have a child and just you know, just give it just what you can manage – but then that's saying that all people who haven't got much money can't have children so that's a bit unfair.
> *Lorna, aged 16*

The ethical dilemma between 'love and money' has some resonance with other values held by young people. For example, the legitimacy given to having sex because you love someone and it appears to be the 'right time', stresses the romantic aspects without thinking out the possible consequences. It may then be 'love' that has accidentally produced a baby whose parents have love available to give it, but little money to support it. Providing materially for a child may come down to either getting a job, or getting benefits like income support and child benefit. This caused another debate that was edged with moral values. Some of the young people considered that the parent(s) should have a job in order to be able to afford everything that a child needed, which for some included clothes and other 'trendy gear'. This was argued about by a group of 15- to 16-year-olds from London.

Rory:	All a child needs is food and love, isn't it?
Jasper:	Yea, but if you can't support ...
Crystal:	Food, clothes, trainers.
Jasper:	No, but still –
Rory:	What they were saying is, right, you've got to be able to work like full time and buy it like all the trendy gear and all that but –
Jasper:	No, not exactly.

In this group it was Candace who quietly suggested that 'You can just go on social.' This, however, is a choice denied to under-16-year-olds by the government, so mothers of this age have little choice other than to get support from their families, and from some other agencies set up by government or the local community to help younger teenage mothers. The question of whether people should be given benefits to support their children proved a hot subject for discussion. Although one Northern Irish group of 15- to 16-year-olds began by asserting that if someone has a child it is their responsibility and they should not take money from anyone else to support it, they eventually acknowledged that some help might be necessary, as long as the parent is the main carer.

Deborah:	It's not fair. It's your child, it's not anybody else's responsibility. You shouldn't be getting money out of anybody else to support it.
Interviewer:	So you don't agree then with child support? What do you think about benefits?
Rowena:	It's sort of like an after thing. You're supporting the child but you need extra help.
Caitriona:	I think you can get money out of relatives and all. Benefits, that's all right.
Rowena:	As long as you're the main carer, the main person,

> I think that's all right. It's always a help to have a bit of help on the side like, that would help the main person.

It seemed to be felt that benefits were the last resort, but they had to be deserved. Being too lazy to work was not condoned.

> If the parents really need help and there's nothing else they can do – they can't get a job – they deserve the money. But if they're just too lazy to go in for a job it's just not fair
> *Geraldine, aged 16*

One group of 14- to 15-year-old Northern Irish young women also considered other avenues of support they saw as open to a struggling parent, such as hostels, and people around to help like nurses and social workers. They also proposed that the baby's grandmother could look after it until the real mother was old enough to do so by getting a job to support the child, but this provoked a heated argument about young people's ability to get jobs.

Aideen:	Well say she was 18 and she still had the wain, her ma could adopt it and then she could look after it when she gets older.
Roma:	Naw, if she's 18, that's different she'd have to look after it herself.
Aideen:	How's it different?
Hayley:	'Cos she would have a job and she could support it then –
Aideen:	And what if she didn't have a job?
Hayley:	Well you should at 18.
Aideen:	How should you at 18, what if you can't get one, what if there's something wrong with you?
Hayley:	Well then you shouldn't have a wain if there's something wrong with you!

The strong moral views asserted by Hayley, that a young person should have a job at 18, belies the situation in many poorer, inner city and rural areas where work is not easy to find. At ages up to 16, and still in school and relatively dependent, young people often have a relatively simple and straightforward moral view about how people should organise their lives – in real life things are usually a lot more complicated. This view covered the ease or difficulty of getting a job and is reflected in assumptions made about combining work and childcare. These young people tended to ignore or neglect the problems and expense involved in obtaining childminders and nursery places. Some thought that a person should look for or get a job if they are going to get pregnant (assuming this is planned), but acknowledged that with a baby you can only go out to work a few hours a day. They had a vague notion of the childcare available for working mothers but no clear knowledge of the real options. Research carried out in the 1990s also endorsed this (Sharpe 1994): most of the young women taking part aspired to various jobs and careers, and simply assumed that when they had children they would continue working and place their child in a nursery.

The young people engaged with either the agenda of supporting a moral stand of going to work, or one against a demonising attitude towards welfare scroungers. On the one hand, the working-class young people generally had more experience of the world of benefits, through their own families. Many came from one-parent families whose mothers were on income support, and they were often more aware of the real need for this kind of support, and also the paucity of job opportunities in the areas in which they lived. On the other hand, many still morally denigrated those who had to resort to benefits and considered that, in general, a person could and should work. The middle-class young people were, if anything, less concerned with this kind of debate. For many, with aspirations to university and a career, this was far enough in the future not to seem very relevant, and probably something that they would not have to address in their own situation. This may or may not be true as, in some areas of work and parts of the country, work is as precarious for professional workers as it is for non-professional ones.

The right age to have children

Lucy:	No I wouldn't have one until I was about twenty-five.
Interviewer:	Is that what you think? Sort of twenty-five?
Lucy:	Twenty-four.
Natalie:	As long as you're married. I would think about having a baby when I was married.
Dougie:	I'd say whenever you want, as long as you've got the stuff to protect them and that there.

14- to 15-year-olds in Northern Ireland

For the young people in the study the right age for having a baby was basically not too young, but not too old. Inasmuch as they gave some support for under-age sex and teenage motherhood, their ideal ages for parenthood were much higher than the teens. For Natalie (quoted above), marriage was seen as a prerequisite, but this is not a view held by the majority. In one group of young people living in the north of

England, everyone said that they wanted to have children. But not very young, they wanted to have a bit of life first, or start a career. For some this might be more difficult, if the pattern in their particular community was for early parenthood and a relatively low level of education. Donna and Sonia considered that by the time a woman was in her 30s she was too old to have children, and certainly too old by the age of 37 (which would exclude someone like Madonna!).

Interviewer:	Do you think it's difficult to have a career and to have kids and –
Donna:	Yea, 'cos then you might not have time for the kids
Sonia:	Yea, might just keep doing it and doing it till you're too old to have a kid.

14- to 15-year-olds in the North of England

In defence of young motherhood, some of the young women in Northern Ireland supported the idea that younger women make better mothers than older women. They considered that their own experiences with younger children in their own families made them more able at mothering.

> I think young women would be better mothers so I do. Look at all those old mothers now, but like us, we're more educated about children and about sex and all too and we know that other people now that are older they didn't know that stuff.
>
> *Aideen, aged 14*

Young people are conscious that 'adults' often put down their level of maturity. Teenage mothers are very aware of being considered by society as being less responsible mothers, and many feel they are stigmatised for this and they often are. Some are constantly trying to prove that they are as good as, or better than, older mothers (Sharpe 1987).

We can understand these views in the context of our earlier discussions of the fragmentation of markers of adulthood and extended economic dependency. Although young people may be sexually active earlier, their ability to support a family may be pushed into the distant future. This process has been paralleled by a movement of women into higher education and employment and a trend towards later childbirth. Commentators have talked about an increasing 'youth divide' with the emergence of diverging paths to adulthood: a growing divide between the minority who start their families in their teens and the majority who are deferring parenthood (Jones 2002). An awareness of this divergence in lifestyle and the difficulties represented by both versions are apparent in these discussions of parenthood. Young people's views on the responsibilities of parenthood and questions of timing are further complicated by their awareness of the fragility of couple relationships and the potential for parenthood to be a solo venture.

'Children need two parents?'

> You should be in a stable relationship – at least at the beginning of a child's life. If – you know, if you've tried to live together and whatever and it just doesn't work out then that's fine – I mean plenty of people get divorced these days – or separate – but at least being in a stable situation to start with and one that you can carry on – don't just have a child with whoever, you don't even know who the child's father is.
>
> *Lorna, aged 16*

Do children really need two parents these days? There are so many one-parent families that maybe this norm is somewhat outdated? This was an issue that came up in various contexts, but it was also the subject of some focus group discussions. In general, while one-parent families were defended as being able to provide adequate parenting support for a child in many cases, it was still seen as the ideal to have two parents around. Once more, this is an issue that has some relationship with social class. It was significant, for instance, that there were far more instances of intact families in our group of middle-class young people, than among those from working-class backgrounds. This does not mean that working-class couples are less able to sustain a relationship, but they often have more material factors working against it, such as poverty and poor housing, which would make it harder for any relationship to survive. Lorna (quoted above) is from a well-off home and has known stability all her life. Young people like Lorna have a better chance of having the material support to look after a child, whether there are two parents or just one. Susannah, also from this area, endorsed the idea that being in a couple provides more grounds for having a child.

> If you're a couple then you've sort of got more argument to have a baby than – you know, if you're on your own you might really want a baby but you're not going to be able to spend enough time with it or working to – you know, you're always going to be struggling but when there's two of you share that responsibility and the baby will, as well, have more of a supportive family.
>
> *Susannah, aged 16*

For one group of 14- to 15-year-olds from Northern Ireland, the fragmentation of

families was common. They generally endorsed a two-parent family, and linked this
with gender and the need for children to relate to a same-sex parent.

Natalie:	I think it's better to have two parents.
Dougie:	I think a wain deserves to have a father.
Natalie:	Say you had a boy and the boy didn't want to talk to the mother, they'd want to talk to –
Dougie:	You'd want two opinions like.
Natalie:	Like the daughter would want to talk to the mother.

The young people in this group compared experiences within their own families,
where their mothers often felt as if they were a single parent through the absence of
help from the father.

> My mum couldn't cope with just me. My dad used to be away a lot on his
> job and my mum just couldn't cope with me on her own, so she looked for
> her mum and dad to help her. And when my dad did come back she had
> him again; and then he went away again and she had two wains to look
> after.
> *Natalie, aged 15*

As a kind of compromise, several young people commented (such as Lorna, quoted
above) that the important thing was that a child had two parents around at the start,
when the child was young, but after that it was less of a problem if they subsequently
broke up. Sixteen-year-old Deborah also endorsed this.

> If they want a child but they're not in a relationship – I don't think that's
> right. They'll be growing up without a parent. If they're in a relationship
> and had a child and then one of them left, it's not as bad.
> *Deborah*

The experiences of several 14- to 15-year-old working-class young women, living on a
rundown estate in the North of England, were of family breakdown, with men
leaving their partners. They did not have a very high opinion of men's ability to stay
in a relationship (Sharpe 2001). They had observed, through their own families and
those of their friends, that it is stressful trying to manage a family without the
support of a man.

Donna:	Sometimes, you know, you'll have the baby and then like the dad or someone will just go and that's when you're left on your own.
Sonia:	And you can't cope with it then –

| Sonia: | Just treat it bad or whatever. |
| Donna: | Just get annoyed with it 'cos it's crying all the time and – |

Parenting can be a tricky subject for discussion. It involves lots of moral overtones about what ought to happen in a family and between parents and children, while in real life it is not so easy to control. Relationships cannot be organised to order. People have children by accident as well as design. Stable relationships become unstable. Many young people are aware of this, although they may not take it into account when thinking of their own future lives and not often when contemplating a sexual relationship. These kinds of consequences can have different effects according to their social and material situations. In general, young people from better-off and more middle-class backgrounds have greater resources in terms of their own family's material and social support than young people from working-class backgrounds. This may affect their present and future educational and occupational opportunities in a radical way. For some young women, having a baby may give them a purpose where there may have been little before, but it also closes many doors – some temporarily, some permanently – and it is often a challenge and a struggle against social isolation and material hardship.

A young person's moral views and knowledge of sex can clearly influence their subsequent sexual relationships and the consequences thereof, which may include pregnancy. Although sex and relationships education is obviously key, their own sense of agency, of controlling and wanting to control this aspect of their lives, is also very important. These young people's views on having children show a mixture of naivety and awareness about the real world of parenthood and, in some cases, strong moral views about possible sources of help. Their views also reflect ambivalence, expressing both the needs and views of the child who desires security, continuity and love, and the emergent adult who desires freedom, respect and fulfilment.

Representations of sex

Another area that gave rise to much debate, discussion and difference of opinion was the representation of sexuality within popular culture. Here we will mainly focus on two forms: first, young women's magazines (and in particular the advice dispensed by agony aunts in problem pages); and second, pornography – a ubiquitous but rarely acknowledged part of young people's sexual cultures, particularly those of young men (Thomson 1999).

Teenage magazines

> ...I've written to a magazine actually and about two years ago I had my story in a problem page and apparently lots of people read it and it was just about boyfriend problems and that that I have and it kind of like made me think – they all make me think about what I'm going to do when I'm older and that and – like so far as I've grown up I reckon my life has changed like just through like listening and reading other people's problems.
> *Andra, aged 13*

> Yea, 'cos girls or boys who've got problems and they don't like talking about it but write to the magazines and then look in it and it gives you – and it tells you the answer to what your problem is.
> *Paula, aged 13*

Sex is represented in magazines in contradictory ways, both as an area for serious reflection and as another aspect of consumption – both information and entertainment (Kehily 2002). There are many magazines for young people, especially young women, such as *Just Seventeen, Bliss, Sugar* and *Shout.* Those writing in them also ascribe values to certain sorts of sex, endorsing the characteristics of 'good sex' and 'bad sex' that were described in earlier sections. For example, they seem to acknowledge the existence of under-age sex but advocate that it should be safe or parent-approved and within a stable relationship.

> Some magazines say you shouldn't be having it under age anyway 'cos like I am fifteen and then the comments on the bottom say you shouldn't be having sex now but some just say as long as you're taking – as long as you're being – having safe sex.
> *Donna, aged 15*

Young people are aware that there is an alternative values regime within which the acceptability of sexual practice could be judged on the basis of physical safety, and this is one that teenage magazines tend to support. The content of magazines in general, but especially their problem pages, serve a vital role as sources of information for young people of both sexes, answering questions that the young people are too scared or embarrassed to ask anyone else. Many of the younger young women in The Respect Study said that they sit together somewhere discussing the issues raised in these pages. In this way, one magazine probably gets a readership of many more than the person who bought it, as these 13-year-olds confirm.

Katie:	I read in my house with all my friends and talk about it.
Jodie:	Whenever I get my magazines I have to give them to one of my friends because she just likes to read them –
Paula:	You sit in the changing rooms in the dinner time talking about everything.

They confirmed magazines as providing them with information about these matters that they would never ask their parents about. It was friends or siblings they confided in most about such issues rather than parents.

> Because you can't talk to your parents if you're under age and you've just had sex so you have to talk to like your mates and your sisters.
> *Sally, aged 14*

Some of The Respect Study young people discussed the statement: 'Teenage magazines are a bad influence on girls' in the focus groups. Overall, they disagreed with this assertion, and considered magazines as providing a lot more useful information, not only about sex but also other personal problems.

> I'm not built like most girls and there's always like problems ... I haven't started growing properly and things like this and when I read about other people's problems and it makes me feel, well, yes, I'm not the only one and that ...
> *Andra, aged 13*

Intimate fears of many kinds like Andra's can be raised and allayed here, such as another young woman's anxiety that she cannot have children because she is late starting her periods, or one who feared that her hip size was unsuitable for childbearing.

Boys and young men also find useful information in the teenage magazines that come their way, especially if they have a sister who buys them. However, they may also use some of this information to tease and embarrass their female peers, as these 13-year-olds describe.

Paula:	Boys look in them just to have a laugh or something over the problem pages 'cos boys think it's dead funny when girls write in –
Jodie:	Yes, 'cos they do that when we're reading in class, just get them out and read them out and say, 'You've got that,' or something like that.
Paula:	They read the problem pages and then ask all the girls,

> 'Oh, does that happen to you? Does that happen to
> you?' Getting dead into it and then you get dead
> embarrassed and they keep going on at you like, 'Oh
> do you have periods?'

Although there was overwhelming support for teenage magazines, there were a few criticisms of some aspects of these publications, or of their moral tones. For example, in the group quoted above, Jodie thought that the ideal images portrayed for young women might influence girls like themselves to become anorexic because they think this is how they should look. Paula described herself as being too thin and said she disliked this aspect of herself as she was only the same skirt size as her seven-year-old sister. Thirteen-year-old Marion, who was rather overweight, was also critical of teenage magazines that write about people being too fat or thin, and then show sylph-like models wearing lovely clothes.

> ... I think sometimes magazines are a bad influence because they show
> people how like pretty girls and everything and then they get really
> depressed about it and go, you know – well, they don't eat or they do eat,
> or they eat too much to become medium size – they're too thin or
> something – I think – it really gets to me (laughs).
> *Marion, aged 13*

Another source of concern to some women, especially the younger ones, was the magazines' general acceptance of abortion as a possible solution to pregnancy, as they thought this might influence the reader to have one.

Some aspects of teenage magazines could also invoke parental disapproval. For example, some young women described how their parents considered them too young for the cosmetic and other 'makeovers' suggested in the magazines. Judy, aged 12, commented that it was her father who disapproved of these, and Josie observed that the magazine girls wear gallons of make-up, short skirts and tiny tops.

Marion, aged 13, voiced more of a moral criticism of teenage magazines for being a bad influence through the contradictory way that the problem pages inform young people that they cannot legally have sex under 16, while the rest of the magazine has many features and advice about sex that seems to condone it. Since girls always read magazines that are aimed at those older than themselves, she thinks it will be the under-16s who are reading about it all. She also objected to the idea of promoting sex as something 'cool', and observed disapprovingly how girls will go and 'do it' at 14 without having a special relationship with the boy. She disagreed with having so much information on sex, asserting such matters are perhaps too complex for the young people reading the magazines, but this was very much a minority view.

Ellie, from one of the older focus groups, reflected how a magazine had in fact exerted some influence on her having sex, but this was not at a very young age.

> The magazines can influence girls to go out and get pregnant. And shag as many boys as humanly possible, you know. It does have that influence. But it's never influenced me to jump into bed with anyone. I do tell a lie – I got to seventeen and opened *Sugar* – the average age for girls losing their virginity was seventeen and three months. Right, two months, let's go and find a man to have intercourse. And I did! Yeah, that might have been my influence for losing my virginity.
> *Ellie, aged 18*

In talking about these kinds of issues, like teenage sex, contraception and pregnancy, everyone, including parents, authorities, and even young people themselves, bemoan the fact that young people do not confide in parents enough about such matters. International evidence suggests that young people in the UK are less likely to be open with their parents about sexual matters than young people in other northern European countries. The reasons for this are likely to be complicated and deeply rooted. Their sexual mentors are friends, siblings, and magazines. Parents generally come well down the list, however keen they are to oblige. Somehow, the family is often a little too close for emotional comfort on some of these issues. Therefore teenage magazines are essentially a benefit for young people and also their parents, in providing information that other sources don't reach. Although they expressed some criticism, most young people, especially the young women, would not be without them, and certainly would not have them reduce or omit their advice and features on sex. They may also provide young people with another viewpoint on such controversial issues, and illustrate the dilemmas and complexities that can be involved. Our data here supports the views of others (Kehily 1999; Bragg and Buckingham 2002) that young people are an active, discerning and self-regulating audience of such representations of sexuality, reading with empathy, scepticism and humour. The moral discourse made available by such magazines is clearly a symbolic resource for young people, and one that can be accepted, resisted and subverted. Rather than focusing on the question of whether or not young people should have access to such material, it would be more pedagogically productive to open these texts up to collective debate and discussion within the sex and relationships education curricula.

Pornography

Debbie:	(Boys) probably wouldn't think that there is anything wrong with it and they wouldn't stop to consider what the girl's views might be.
Anne:	It's like abusing the girl's rights.
Vicky:	Yea, but girls want to do it though, don't they?
Debbie:	Not all of them.
Vicky:	Yea, but some of them. They wouldn't – they'd do it for the money and I'd rather be homeless than actually do pornography.

12- to 13-year-olds

A different but related aspect of sexual representation is the depiction of people, usually women, in pornographic images portrayed in magazines, films or videos. In the value judgements part of The Respect Study questionnaire, young people were asked to judge the activity of 'reading or watching pornography'. There was a somewhat polarised response, which was also gendered. Two in five (40 per cent) of the young people (33 per cent of the boys and 47 per cent of the girls) thought that it was 'always' or 'usually wrong'; 17 per cent were 'not sure', and a third (33 per cent) of the boys and 16 per cent of the girls said that it was 'rarely' or 'never wrong'. Therefore, although the majority disapproved, a significant number showed some approval, especially amongst the boys.

This topic was discussed in more detail in some of the focus groups, with the statement 'Pornography is just a laugh.' A number of gender differences similarly emerged here. The most obvious was that, while pornography was acknowledged to be a 'laugh' for boys, it was generally disliked and disapproved of by girls who did not find it a laugh – although some found some boys' reactions to it to be laughable. Anne thought that it was a reflection on men themselves.

> Some people think that men looking at women is just a part of growing up but it's not – some people are like completely obsessed with it and it's disgusting. I mean I went into a newsagent about three weeks ago and I just saw these men looking at these magazines and it changes your view on men sometimes – it's just so disgusting.
> *Anne, aged 13*

Diane criticised naked girls being on car advertisements, and how this was not considered to be pornography.

> I know some boys read car magazines and sometimes they have these naked women advertising these alloy wheels and they don't look at it as pornography but, as you say, it's just a laugh – and they go 'Wow! She's nice,' and they start comparing it to girls in their class
>
> *Diane, aged 13*

Vicky and Jenny thought that although boys claim to approve of porn, if you push them they don't really, it is more their conformity to peer pressure.

> Vicky: Some boys do actually think it's really wrong because they just think it is absolutely disgusting to do because if you go up to a boy in the playground they'll say, 'Oh, yea' – and then they'll say, 'No, I don't really' – they do it for – they say 'Yea' for a joke, and then they say, 'No, I think it's absolutely wrong.'
>
> Jenny: I think a lot of boys do it 'cos they have like an image 'cos their mates think it's cool and they have to 'cos they've got an image.
>
> *12- to 13-year-olds*

In an older mixed sex group in the same school, young women were in the majority, and monopolised this particular discussion, while the two young men remained very quiet. It was left to some of the young women to suggest that young men said or acted as if they liked pornography in order to conform or fit in. The young men were mainly reduced to silence or, in one case, a young man spoke nervously, shaking his head: 'I don't know – I know some mates who have looked at it but I know – I don't know if any girls looked at it, I don't know ... ' It embarrassed them when they were actually put on the spot about it in the company of young women.

Reactions to seeing pornography are also gendered. For example, it is the turn of young women to get embarrassed if it is on the television for example, especially in the company of young men. But they also generally think it's 'sad' that the young men are getting pleasure looking at female naked bodies.

> My sister's boyfriend brother was over in our house, and it was about one o'clock on a Friday night and we were just sitting there and we were watching TV and it was on Sky and we were just sitting there flicking the channels and porn came on, you know REALLY really dirty, I was all 'get that there over', and he was all 'Nah, like keep it here, keep it here' and he was just sitting there watching it away and I just had to go out then.
>
> *Aileen, aged 14*

But there was some dissent from the idea that all girls disapprove of pornography. In another group, Elsa and Amanda defined a certain kind of girl who did not like these images, and they thought personality was more relevant than gender.

Interviewer:	Do you think boys and girls have different opinions on pornography?
Elsa:	Girly girls really hate it ...
Amanda:	Yea, girly girls.
Interviewer:	What are girly girls?
Elsa:	Girls who are like – girls scream and never swear and like always brush their hair and – I'm not saying that like girly girls – other girls don't brush their hair but, you know, like bring hair brushes into school, make sure they're absolutely immaculate.
Amanda:	Do everything right.
Elsa:	And giggle –
Amanda:	It depends what sort of person you are. I don't think it's girls and boys – I think it's like what sort of person you are.

13- to 14-year-olds

Some young women suggested, by way of excuse or explanation, that the women posing for the pictures or films may enjoy being looked at, but others considered this to be an exploitation of women. In the context of exploitation, some young people suggested that women might be bribed into being involved. Several could not comprehend how a woman could actually choose to do this 'work'.

I think it's just stupid putting your – having like loads of people seeing you naked just for money – I mean there's plenty of other jobs, you don't just have to do that.

Hazel, aged 14

But money does play an important part, and 16-year-old Andrew and Keith were more aware of this.

Andrew:	If it was just a laugh then how come there's so much money involved?
Keith:	It's just a business isn't it, I suppose.

There are a few 'soft' pornographic magazines for women that portray pictures of naked men in provocative poses. This seems to embarrass both sexes, but more so the young men. They get very uncomfortable if they are shown images of naked men, while many young women, like Diane, find them simply boring or rather funny.

> I don't know, I don't want to compare a man to a woman or anything – I don't even like to look at naked people – but there's a lot more in a woman's body to look at than a man's. I mean (laughs) there's nothing about a man really that is particularly attractive. (laughter) No, you just see this – it's so boring!
> *Diane, aged 13*

As in various other issues under discussion, such as having sex, relationships and marriage, young people do not want to be simply told what to believe or do, and this extended to values around pornography in that some young women as well as young men considered that if pornography 'is not harming anyone, it's OK'. They asserted the individual's right to choose either to be involved in posing for porn, or whether to look at it.

> I think it's kind of up to them really 'cos if that's the type of thing they want to do then that's fine and it's a personal opinion because if that's what they like doing them.
> *Elsa, aged 14*

What some of the young women in The Respect Study disliked were the comparative implications. They thought they would not mind so much about boyfriends looking at pornography, but they would object if these young men started comparing them and their bodies to the women in these films or magazines. Once more it is the 'ideal' images set up, which women have historically found it difficult or impossible to compete with, that continue to have an effect.

> Sheila: If you're sitting with a group of boys you know in a room and say they have –
>
> Aileen: – and something dirty comes on TV they all start laughing and all.
>
> Bridget: They say look at the state of her compared to her, the wee girl's [*demonstrates something + laughter*] and you run ...
>
> *13- to 14-year-olds*

There were a few positive views on pornography voiced by young people who thought that it could have a function if it distracted men away from actually acting in a sexual way towards women, or even from going out and sexually assaulting or raping a woman. But this was an arguable assertion and others would contend that it could fire up a man's desire and promote some kind of female sexual harassment or abuse.

Some young people brought up the issue of child pornography, but this was in a different league for them. It was viewed as very bad, as 'sick', it was considered much worse than adult pornography and some related it to child abuse. In Britain we seem to have a rather contradictory attitude to sexuality, which simultaneously represses and incites (Epstein and Johnson 1998). Young children are not meant to be 'sexual' but the attention that is paid to people who prey on them, that is abusers and paedophiles, serves to sexualise them. This attitude is likely to fuel the attraction of child pornography, which has become more accessible to those seeking it, through the facilities of the internet.

Pornography is often seen as serving to exploit women's bodies. It is the male gaze on a woman's naked form that aims to use her sexuality to turn him on, fuelled by a man's own conditioning and peer influence. As we have seen, pornography fits into a set of related sexual values, which also includes sexism, something implicit in pornography. The young women were predictably more condemnatory about 'sexism' in the questionnaire's moral judgement items than young men, although both sexes were mainly disapproving. A total of 74 per cent considered sexism to be 'always/usually wrong' – 81 per cent of young women and 68 per cent of the young men. Few (6 per cent) thought it was acceptable, that is, 'rarely/never wrong'. In terms of a concept of 'good' and 'bad' sexual issues or activities, sexism is seen as 'bad'.

However, sexism is something that is also perpetuated to some extent through jokes, as evidenced when the young people were asked in the questionnaire to tell a joke or a funny story that was going around at the moment. Of the 661 who did so, 88 (13 per cent) gave one that had some kind of sexual content. The proportions were about the same for both the young men and the young women (14 per cent and 12 per cent respectively). We classified these jokes into general categories. Those with a sexual type of content in fact made up the largest single category, followed by 'tits, bums, and willies' (9 per cent). As might be expected, this genre consisted mainly of 'dirty jokes' (52 per cent) and sexist ones (19 per cent). The two sexes produced quite similar proportions, and perhaps surprisingly, a slightly higher percentage of young women than young men produced 'dirty jokes'. The selection of jokes that follow are illustrative of an underlying sexual discourse that is available in the young people's social culture, especially school.

Whether or not some young people (especially younger ones) totally understand their content, or their implications, sexist or otherwise, they are a representation of sex, and like pornography, an informal form of sex and relationships education. A number of the jokes from the Northern Ireland schools were understandably couched in a religious context.

> Q: What's the difference between a Lada and Pamela Anderson?
> A: At least you feel a real tit when your in a Lada.
> *Young man, 15–16, Northern Ireland*

> Q: Two nuns in a bath. Which one is the alcoholic?
> A: The one with the black bush.
> *Several young people, 15–16, Northern Ireland*

> Q: What's the difference between life and a man's penis?
> A: Life's always hard.
> *Young woman, 15–16, Northern Ireland*

> Q: What's the speed limit during sex?
> A: 68, because at 69 you have to turn round.
> *Young woman, 15–16, Northern Ireland*

> Q: How do you circumcise a priest?
> A: Slap the altar boy on the back of the head.
> *Young man, 12–13, Northern Ireland*

An old lady lived with her poodle, Timmy. One day she found a wishing stone. She wished to be rich, to be young, and for Timmy to be a handsome man. 'Timmy is that really you?' she exclaimed when she saw him. 'Yes' he said, 'and aren't you mad you had me neutered!'
Young woman, 11–12, English school

> Q: Why did the pervert cross the road?
> A: He had his willy stuck in a chicken.
> *Young woman, 11–12, English school*

> Q: What did the hurricane say to the coconut tree?
> A: Hold on to your nuts, it's not a normal blow job.
> *Young woman, 11–12, English school*

> Q: How many Essex girls does it take to change a light bulb?
> A: They don't: they screw in Cortinas!
> *Young man, 14–15, English school*

> Two nuns sitting on a bench and a streaker runs past. One nun has a
> stroke and the other couldn't quite reach.
> *Young man, 15–16, English school*

Although both young men and young women may know and enjoy these kinds of
jokes, it is probably young women more than young men who will find them less
funny as they grow older and become more aware of the implicit or explicit sexism
that is often involved.

As a form of sexism, pornography emerges as being generally a 'bad' thing, more
especially frowned on by young women than young men, but demonstrates how its
appeal continues through the male generations, in spite of feminism and the
increased assertiveness of young women. But what has also been shown from
research is that pornography is a major source of sexual information for young men
who fail to get this either from their family or school sex and relationships education
(Hilton 2003; Measor and others 2000). As such, its 'value' in this sense should not
be ignored. Perhaps, if pornography is an inevitable source of information for some
young men, there may be some way of acceptably harnessing this in formal sex and
relationships education. However, it is not the form of sexuality that encourages
respect for young women, nor gains young men respect from young women for
watching it. Many of the young women in The Respect Study were very deprecating
about the kind of people they assumed looked at it. 14-year-old Diana considered
pornography to be just for perverts, or men who don't have or can't get a girlfriend.
She thought they must be pretty desperate to look at pictures. But there were also
others who asserted the individual's rights to look at what they wanted.

> Well, I found my brother's porno mags when I was playing with his
> computer and I felt a bit sorry for him actually but I mean – it's 'cos I
> don't like reading porno mags but it's not really any of my business – he's
> much older – but I guess if they want it it's fine.
> *Elsa, aged 14*

Most popular discussions of pornography focus on the question of whether it is
morally acceptable or not, giving rise to responses informed by conservative, liberal
and feminist arguments. The young people's discussions (above) reflect these wider
cultural narratives. Although pornography is generally not targeted at teenagers in
the same explicit way as young women's magazines, it nevertheless constitutes an
important part of teenage sexual culture. Most young people come into contact with
pornographic imagery, and they must make sense of it. In so doing, they must
negotiate the relationship between representations of a particular form of adult

sexuality and their own emergent sense of themselves as sexual beings. Pornography is also associated with homosocial culture (that is, associating in same sex groups, for example boys mixing with boys) and can be understood as playing a part in drawing boundaries between the culture of boys and men, and that of mixed company (Thomson 1999). As can be seen from the above, an open discussion of pornography gives rise to spirited debates concerning agency, gender, desire, fantasy and human rights. In our view, the same educational case can be made for opening up pornographic texts for discussion and debate within sex and relationships education as can be made for teenage magazines.

Homosexuality

Homosexuality was the subject of various aspects of The Respect Study. When the young people talked about homosexuality, it was in relation to people being gay or lesbian. One subject that never came up spontaneously, and was not asked about by the researchers, was bisexuality, although this is another equally important alternative to heterosexuality. In this study, the questionnaire responses showed moral judgements on homosexuality that usually indicate high levels of homophobia, which stood awkwardly apart from the responses to other sex-related values (such as attitudes towards pornography, under-age sex and sexism) and from other 'life issues' (such as attitudes towards abortion, euthanasia, suicide and cloning), both of which hang together with a certain pattern and logic (see Thomson 2000). Attitudes towards homosexuality seem to play quite a specific role. The young people's responses differed by gender and, to some extent, age (for young women), religion, social class and location. (Details of the questionnaire responses concerning homosexuality have been described earlier in *Patterns in sexual values*, page 7.)

Despite a movement towards increasingly tolerant interpersonal values, many young people continue to be confused and uncomfortable about non-heterosexual identities. Attitudes towards same sex sexual relations are historically and culturally variable. It has been argued that 'heterosexuality' and 'homosexuality' as currently understood are relatively new, and that the negative constructions of homosexuality are integral to positive constructions of heterosexuality (Weeks, 1989). Contemporary studies have revealed the high levels of homophobia in schools and other areas inhabited by young people (for example, Epstein 1996, 1997; Nayak and Kehily 1996, 1997; Mac An Ghaill 1994; O'Donnell and Sharpe 2000; Frosh and others 2001).

The issue of homosexuality is an important subject that has been generally excluded from school sex and relationships education programmes, and young people's views on this have been given a fair amount of space in this thinkpiece. It is hoped that they can be useful in promoting sensitive and fruitful discussion in the face of the continuing homophobia that permeates community spaces inhabited by young people, such as schools.

Young people and homophobia

If, as has been suggested by various researchers (Nayak and Kehily 1996; Frosh and others 2001) homophobia is to do with policing gender identities rather than to do with sexuality, this reflects the rigidity of masculine identities for young men. For example, while young women may be able to experiment with and appropriate aspects of masculinity (such as playing football, being 'hard', adopting male fashions, and so on) young men do not find it safe or easy to play with equivalent aspects of femininity. Homophobia among young people plays a major part in enforcing gender conformity, and thus to the construction of heterosexuality. It is often enacted within a same-sex group, a homosocial activity that contributes to confirming and enforcing a strongly heterosexual stance. And to a large extent, 'homosexuality' is just a word to young people who have no experience of gay or lesbian people. It is a label rather than an assertion of sexual identity.

As well as The Respect Study focus groups conducted within the various schools, several focus groups were conducted with non-school based groups, including a gay and lesbian group who were mainly 17 to 18 years old. Most of the young people's views on homosexuality were given in response to contentious statements under discussion in focus groups: 'Homosexuality is normal' or 'Homosexuality is just a phase', and sometimes the subject came up incidentally under another statement. In the school-based groups, young people of both sexes gave generally negative reactions to these statements about homosexuality. For example, they expressed the popular prejudice that homosexuality is not 'normal' or 'natural'. Despite some more liberal judgements in the questionnaire responses, there was general agreement with the following views.

> Say if you walk down the street and you see two lesbians or gays it's your natural reaction to go – Urgh! – you know.
> *Yasmin, aged 14*

> (I think it's not normal) because the main majority of people aren't like it.
> *Carol, aged 16*

It was often the perceived 'unnatural' nature of the physical sexual aspects of gay or lesbian relationships that bothered the young people, such as two people of the same sex kissing. Although religion rarely entered young people's moral discourse elsewhere, another familiar argument against homosexuality was that this contradicts the belief that God made man and woman to reproduce, and some young people spoke against what they saw as the inappropriate nature of gay parenting.

> But it's not right. Because these are people, but they've got a child, two gay people like they've got a child and they look after it. Like I don't think that'll be the right environment to bring up a child in.
> *Donovan, aged 16*

For most young people in the early/mid teens, homosociality is the norm – in general, boys mix with boys and girls mix with girls. At this stage in their lives, homophobia may be instrumental in managing their homosocial relationships, and promoting the development of heterosexuality. It is different for boys and girls.

Homophobia for boys and young men

Homophobia among boys is a well documented feature of school life, and Epstein (1996, 1997) has described how boys who did not behave in an 'appropriately' macho way were often victims of this form of sexism, expressed in terms of their supposed similarities to girls. Connell (1995) has theorised homosexuality as 'subordinate masculinity' on the grounds that it is a form of masculinity that attracts widespread disapproval and even persecution. 'Femininity' in a boy or man – which is how homosexuality is often stereotyped – is for many boys the unacceptable 'enemy within' masculine identity itself. High levels of homophobia emerged in The Respect Study focus groups and in some of the interviews, and reflected a need to be constantly enforcing gender boundaries.

Boys police their identities by constructing other boys as transgressing gender boundaries. They are very concerned with the popular ways of being boys, and loud, sports-playing personalities tended to be seen as the 'popular' group, while quieter, non-sporty, studious boys could be targets for this homophobia (O'Donnell and Sharpe 2000; Frosh and others 2001). Boys are very conscious of what they can acceptably say and do if they are to remain within these boundaries. For example, two women holding hands would not provoke much attention, but two men certainly would. Similarly, girls can compliment each other's appearance, but boys cannot, as Dermot observed.

> Aye, they might think (he's good looking) but they're feared to say it in case anybody thinks something about them. They might think it into themselves but that's all they could do really.
>
> *Dermot, aged 15*

Anything associated with femininity, even affection, is to be denigrated in the constant reinforcing of their masculine identities. Lee, aged 14, even considered that it would be inappropriate to have something like 'boy power', in the same way as we have had 'girl power', because 'It don't sound right, it sounds too girlish – it sounds too gayish.'

Boys may also apply gender boundaries to girls and be hostile to girls they choose to consider or call a lesbian. Della, now aged 17, had discovered she was lesbian when she was in her teens and still at school, and found it was the boys more than girls who reacted negatively.

Other young people in the study endorsed this gendered reaction.

> Definitely boys are more homophobic than the girls are, I don't know, I suppose it's a type of prejudice but ... boys think of it as a lot more sort of degrading than girls. Girls think, oh, it's just part of life really whereas boys think it's a bit, to be gay, it's a bit ... if someone says, 'Oh ... gay' it's considered almost as an insult whereas girls would be like 'Oh, why ... ' and if someone was gay and people were joking about it, girls would be more 'Don't be sort of like that, it's not their fault, it's just ... '
>
> *Roger, aged 16*

There may have been some liberalisation of attitudes to homosexuality among boys, reflecting the growth of identity politics over recent decades, but it is very slow. Such a loosening of traditional masculinity means a threat to its power and privilege, and some boys may feel the need to define and assert their masculine identities even more strongly. There is a never-ending struggle to achieve some 'real' masculinity that cannot be sustained.

In O'Donnell and Sharpe's research (2000), a few young men could express more liberal views in private, but they agreed that it would be foolish to seem sympathetic to homosexuality when they were amongst 'the boys', because of all the barracking they would get. Despite their schools' strong endorsement of anti-sexist policies, the negative attitudes and treatment between pupils of anyone thought to be homosexual, or the use of homosexual labels as terms of abuse, did not appear to be actively addressed. As Harry observed of his homophobic friends: 'They're happy to say racism is disgusting and should be stamped out, yet they won't appreciate it's the same sort of subject, along the same lines.' But it is hard to counter these levels of homophobia when it appears to be a marker of emergent masculinity and a significant feature of identity formation among boys.

Homophobia for girls and young women

Interviewer:	And do you have any lesbians in class?
All:	Not that we know of. (laughter)
Interviewer:	What would happen if there were? How would they be seen or treated?
Yasmin:	I suppose if everyone found out they'd be bullied.
Jane:	Yea, they would be bullied.
Lola:	I wouldn't go in the same changing room as them though.

14- to 15-year-olds

The Respect Study young people voiced several popular misconceptions about the nature of homosexuality. One was that they tended to endorse the stereotyped view that gays and lesbians present a threat to heterosexuals. They assumed that gay people are looking to approach and try to seduce straight people. In their discussions this was more openly apparent with the girls than the boys. It was the girls who spoke in more detail about their feelings about lesbians than boys did about gay men. Many of the boys and young men simply spoke of homosexuality as being unnatural or disgusting and did not encourage any real discussion about it, possibly because any show of interest or concern could be interpreted as an implication of sympathy or gayness in themselves. The young women's fears were not generally based on any personal contact with lesbian or gay young people but on hearsay and stereotype, and their hypothetical reaction was panic. Some 13- to 14-year-old girls spoke of their fears that lesbians will 'try it on' with them.

Lola:	Would you hang about with a lesbian though? I'd be scared.
Jane:	Yea, I don't know – it depends how long you've known them.
Lola:	Yea, but just – what would you do? – Like I'd be scared just in case –

Jane:	What, if she said to me, I'm a lesbian? (laughs)
Lola:	Yea, but like if she was your best friend and you was talking like and you went to her, oh, come up to my bedroom or something and you were sitting there and she, you know – (laughs) tried it on with you I'd be scared.
Jane:	Yea, if she tried it on I'd kill her.

14- to 15-year-olds

Estelle also had a very predatory view of lesbian behaviour.

> No, it's just that, the thing is, lesbian's scare me – because I'm straight
> and everything and I think that's the expression, and if a lesbian came
> up to you and started chatting you up, you'd freak – and you'd run to
> the next per–, the person next to you and say: 'Hi' – you know, you
> could, you'd just sort of like start talking to them as if to say: 'Oh I'm
> taken.'

Estelle, aged 14

Estelle and the others reveal the limits of their way of understanding (homo) sexuality. For them a lesbian appears like a 'Trojan horse', containing the 'enemy within', in a similar way to Nayak and Kehily's (1996) suggestion that femininity is the 'enemy within' for young men. These young women are inferring male sexuality onto lesbian women, assuming they might behave like the worst kind of pushy men. Seeing lesbians as sexual predators eclipses the more individualised rights-based approach, in which difference is accepted or tolerated, that characterises many young women's views on many other 'sexual values' issues.

Girls' and young women's friendships with each other are a key aspect of their lives, and friendship-related problems and tensions came up repeatedly in interviews and also featured frequently in the dilemmas they defined in the questionnaire. Their concerns around their sexuality are increased by the anxiety that their friendships could be sexual. They are uncertain what their feelings for other girls may mean. This creates tension between homosociality and homosexuality – between friendship and sexuality. As described in 'Representations of sex' (page 57), the possible feminising of sexuality is reflected in their approach to the problem pages of girls' magazines for advice on this subject, and for confirmation of another common belief among girls, that liking/being attracted to other girls is a temporary phase. For girls, having a 'crush' on a teacher or an older girl is nothing new. In her research on girls' friendships, Valerie Hey (1997) noted the undercurrents of sexuality in some of their relationships. In this context, girls' feelings for other girls or women can be questioned or dismissed as 'just a phase'.

Lindsay:	'Cos (in the problem pages) it's like 'I think I fancy a girl' and 'Am I a lesbian?'
Terese:	And then it says like, 'You go through this at your age' and then you think, oh, I wonder if I might go through it ...
Lindsay:	They say everyone has to go through a stage like that – I don't!

12- to 13-year-olds

The homophobic discourses expressed by young men and women depend on constructing a person as a category, rather than as real. In order to start undermining these, there has to be an opposing moral discourse about friendship and about living with or accepting difference. If they (knowingly) had friendly contact with people who are gay or lesbian, their fears may have been somewhat allayed. Their anticipated responses were mainly based on it being gay strangers that they might encounter, rather than people that they knew, which might be a different experience, as Roger, aged 16, implied.

> See there's no point we know to get into an encounter with gays, so we wouldn't know how to treat it. Like if one of my friends was to turn around to say they were gay it would be a lot different to if a stranger was to say it.
> *Roger*

This was endorsed by Lorna in her group discussion.

> If I said to you – 'Susannah I've got a feeling I might be gay' – you wouldn't laugh at me and go – 'Oh, get away from me, I might catch it' ...
> *Lorna, aged 16*

The homophobia expressed by boys differs from that expressed by girls, as illustrated in The Respect Study research. But both homophobic discourses are predicated on dehumanising gays and lesbians. They have to be seen as the enemy, as strangers, and not as someone they could know and even like. Several young people suggested that not knowing anyone who is gay or lesbian can allow fears and fantasies to develop through ignorance. As soon as they start to know or meet a gay person or have a relative who is gay, these attitudes show their brittleness and begin to crack under the strain of personal experience, creating space for an alternative discourse.

Creating other perspectives

The media has contributed to an increased visibility of homosexuality. Some young people suggested that the portrayal of gay people in areas of the media – as comperes, and on chat shows, and as characters portrayed in soap operas – help to make homosexuality more acceptable. It represents another way of 'knowing' someone vicariously. But 16-year-old Francis was less sure: 'If you see it on TV, you accept it, because people are only on TV, but in real life it's sort of different.' Nevertheless, having visual images, for example, seeing and possibly getting familiar with and 'involved' with the complex lives of gay or lesbian characters on regular television soap operas can serve to challenge and confound the simplicity of homophobia. Since this prejudice works through dehumanising and silencing or repressing humanity, there is a relationship between such visibility and acceptance.

Amidst the homophobia, there were some voices in the study trying to at least discuss the issue and put forward a more liberal and egalitarian view. These tended to be the older young people and the young women, but not exclusively so. In so doing, they also revealed contradictions between the homophobia they had become used to at school, and some of their emerging liberal notions. This sometimes included discussion of what might make people gay or lesbian – whether it is a matter of nature, social environment or choice?

Could it be nature – perhaps something to do with hormones, as Richard was considering?

> It could be their hormones as well – apparently they've got like more hormones or something – more female hormones – 'cos some gay people do actually look like women – they actually look more female than male ... I reckon.
> *Richard, aged 16*

Sixteen-year-old Sam 'came out' to the researcher in his second interview, yet at his first interview he had not yet recognised that he was gay. Here he expressed a mixture of beliefs about the origins of one's sexuality identity.

> I don't think you're born that way. No, society makes your personality. You don't exactly get your personality when you're a little kid, when you're a baby. It's when you grow up ... You don't just grow up and think – right, I'll be gay ... It could be like – if like you're a woman trapped in a man's body or something.
> *Sam, aged 16*

Some also questioned the effects of social circumstances in which children grow up, and talked of whether boys playing with dolls, or growing up with a lot of girls rather than boys could affect them in this way.

In one group of 15- to 16-year-olds, it was observed that because being gay or lesbian could cause a lot of problems, homosexuality was unlikely to be a choice because the easier option would be to be straight.

> But it is just like the way some people are, 'cos I don't think there's many people who would like choose to be gay in this society – like the amount of prejudice there is – if you want to go for an easy life then you probably just – if you could choose – be straight 'cos it would just take the pressure off you.
>
> *Susannah, aged 16*

In the same discussion, Lorna disputed that being gay or lesbian was a phase.

> 'Cos I mean if you just take people that are gay ... people who are gay all their lives and if it was just a phase then they wouldn't be with a man or a woman and a woman if it was just a phase then.
>
> *Lorna, aged 16*

Some young people were critical of the treatment of gay and lesbian young people, and expressed the difficulties of coming to terms with this.

> I think it's, I dunno, whatever makes you happy I suppose. It's just really hard to come to terms with. I think if you don't know someone that's gay then you're really ignorant to the fact. It's like once you get to know them, they're the same as (us).
>
> *Carol, aged 16*

It is significant that those young people who move beyond a homophobic discourse engage in this way with questions of 'causality', which concern the relative fixity or fluidity of sexual identity. Tensions between understandings of sexual identity – as fixed or constructed – have been discussed by Waites in exploring how medical and psychological understandings of sexual identity as being fixed at 16, have dominated public debates over equalising the age of consent in the UK in the 1990s (Waites 2003). He finds that choice in sexual identity is emphasised within sexual politics and more popular media representations. Choice or its absence has a compelling moral subtext. The adoption of a naturalised or fixed model of sexual identity fits well with liberal moral discourses of equality, in which difference is placed beyond choice – 'it's not their fault', and thus inequality is unfair. In contrast, an approach that emphasises choice in sexual identity moves discussions into the more contested moral territory occupied by issues such as abortion, euthanasia and cloning, which can be viewed as 'messing with the natural order'. Questions of sexual identity are poised at the intersection of these two moral discourses in a way that is both challenging and potentially productive. In this light, it makes sense to encourage young people, in any discussion around these questions of sexual identity, to explore and expand on any interest they express in issues of causality.

Experiences of gay and lesbian young people

> I was very happy when I came out. Finally I realised what it was about me.
> *Della, aged 17*

One of The Respect Study focus groups was made up of 17- to 18-year-olds who had all come out as gay or lesbian. Like their 'straight' peers, their experiences had been framed by homophobic attitudes, growing up in the same environment and with the same prejudices. The process of having to distance themselves from these identities is very individualising. They have to try and fit themselves into these powerful discourses with which they are so at odds, such as the perceptions about homosexuality involving predatory behaviour, or being something contagious. In the end, they usually cannot fit in, and leave school and often home as well. They have to try and find a human identity for themselves through the denial of the homophobic 'inhumanity' they have grown up with, and embark on their own project of self.

When Devon, now aged 17, realised that he was gay, it came as something of a shock. He had already felt very isolated in his self-questioning, but what made it more complicated was that he himself had the residue of a lot of the homophobic attitudes that young men grow up with.

> I know I was homophobic when I was fourteen ... I was thinking that no, it's completely unnatural. I really did think I was the only person in the world who had that problem, because I'd heard about someone being gay, but I never actually thought there were people out there, who were like that. So I thought that gay was just an expression. I didn't think they existed at that age and I was just like, NO! NO WAY! NO WAY! I thought it was like a disease you – not a disease, but like a – a thing that you shouldn't be thinking. A thing that should be got rid of ...
> *Devon*

When he did come to recognise himself as gay, Devon was understandably very cautious about the possible reactions of his school classmates to any hint of homosexuality. Young people who know or suspect that they are not heterosexual are well aware of the attitudes and anxieties that this engenders in others. Indeed, some may have taken on and expressed these attitudes quite vehemently themselves. And as we have heard from some of the young women quoted earlier, the views they expressed about supposed predatory lesbians would make any young woman think twice before admitting even any confusion about her sexual identity.

Della, 17 at the time of the interview, had realised she was lesbian when she was still at school but, like Devon, had felt very isolated. She was amazed when she discovered some time later that other young people had had similar experiences at this young age or even younger.

> I thought, how can anyone else (like) this young know now, I thought it was strange that I knew early, so early. And now I've met people who were younger than me and now I'm getting older ... I mean they're not that much younger than me – but it actually makes me think that I'm not the youngest any more.
> *Della*

It is the isolation that can be very hard for emerging young gay men and women and Devon commented.

> I always wish I did have the influence of a gay person when I was coming to terms with, er, with myself, but as far as I know, I'm the only one in my family.
> *Devon*

Young people who are being picked on at school for any reason can lose a lot of confidence. While Della had decided to leave school and home (because her parents were not very understanding) to find a more supportive environment, she was perhaps unusual in that she also developed enough confidence in herself as a gay young woman to eventually confront the name-callers at school.

> I used to be called – like there's an expression that – that they always give girls at school if they've got short hair – and dress boyish – they – what is it? Geezerbird, something like that. So they used to call me that and I – I don't know why but I got satisfaction out of turning round and saying, 'No, actually I'm a dyke.' And the look on their faces of shock, that I'd actually said it, was like, it was so satisfying to see that shock on their face and see

that they were speechless. Erm, and half the time they didn't actually say anything about it afterwards.

Della

Young people who realise they are gay, lesbian or bisexual feel very vulnerable in all areas of life but especially with their family and friends, and if they are in school or college. What they need is some support and recognition of the validity and value of their feelings, but what they encounter often falls far short of this. Parents can have a mixed reaction and if they cannot come to terms with the situation, the relationships may be lost or tainted. Like Della, many young people leave home for somewhere more accepting and anonymous, like London, where they can find like-minded people where they exist. Gay and lesbian youth groups and similar organisations have gone a long way in providing them with essential support.

Young people like Devon and Della are not just responding to homophobia but are attempting to build positive identities. Initially they try and make sense of themselves in relation to these highly negative images of homosexuality, and may struggle with feelings arising from such pathologised versions of the self. Often they will remove themselves from the homophobic beliefs and attitudes that they have been brought up with, and ultimately make sense of and reject them as unjust and uninhabitable. In practice, this may mean that they drop out of education because their situation is incompatible with the fiercely heterosexual institution that is the school.

I just felt like the whole world was against me – at one stage, so I just thought, if the whole world's against me, fuck the world. And that meant fuck school and everything else. So I think that was just I just didn't care about anything else, I just – I wanted to be who I was, and explore it really.

Della

Homophobia is as much about heterosexual policing as it is about lesbians and gays. Homosexual identities and heterosexual identities are both problematic. There is not a strong line between homosexual and heterosexual cultures and people have ambivalent desires. One problem is the ongoing fragility of heterosexuality. All the energy that goes into expressing homophobia signals that this is something that needs much working on and through. The negative reaction of the girls and young women expressed earlier is a good example, and the apparent vicarious pleasure they seem to experience in imagining what they might do if they were in a 'situation' with a lesbian.

For young people who are developing their identities, homosexuality has to be addressed very carefully and sensitively (Forrest and others 1997). Concerns, confusion, anxieties, and insights about being gay or lesbian are very present in schools, but mainly invisible. They are hard to address by pupils or teachers in a way that will positively benefit the issue or the people concerned. Young people are aware of a social change towards individual choice, for example, people can now pursue a variety of careers in their lifetime, and they can marry or live together, so why should not people have a choice of sexualities? At present this appears far too threatening, although Giddens (1992, 1999) sees the development of gay and lesbian relationships as a positive marker for future change.

For those young people who are grappling with the recognition (private or public) of the nature of their sexuality, their experiences and identities are often profoundly affected by the cultural context in which homophobia takes place. Young gays and lesbians themselves have to exert their own individuality against their 'inhuman' labels and are often forced to seek a more 'comfortable' existence away from home. In this context, sexual bullying is one aspect of bullying in school that has been receiving some well-needed attention (Douglas and others 1997; Warwick and Douglas 2000).

Conclusion

The issues under discussion in this section were ones which tended to provoke strong moral opinions and feelings, and often polarised the young people according to gender, ethnicity, religion, social class, and sometimes location.

Abortion, parenting, and to some extent homosexuality, were areas that tended to be modified with increasing age, observation of others' situations and dilemmas, and personal experience. Abortion was quite strongly linked to religious beliefs and commitment, but also related to social class, whereby those from a working-class background were more accepting of early parenthood and put having a baby (or conversely not 'killing' it through abortion) ahead of the educational, career or other aspirations of a pregnant young woman. For the middle-class (and also some aspiring working-class) young people in the study, such aspirations were clearly of importance, and both young men and women recommended a later age for having children so that they could do something with their lives first. Similarly, it was the working-class young people who put 'love' as the necessary and often sufficient component of parenting, while there were mixed feelings and arguments about the need for financial and material support and the necessity of having a job. The need for having two parents to bring up children was also linked to class and community values, for example in the working-class location in the North of

England, a one-parent family was the norm and it was not a stigma to be in one, even if two parents were preferred as ideal. Many young women in this location were sceptical about the likelihood of men staying around in a family relationship.

The representation of sex and sexual values was very much a gender issue, in which teenage magazines served a vital purpose in helping young women through the questions and phases that they would be reluctant to bring to the attention of their parents, and to some extent gave some insights to young men who also accessed these publications. In contrast, pornography, although playing some role in 'educating' young men about the mechanics of sex, albeit not the dynamics of 'love', is denigrated by young women (and some young men) for its sexist portrayal of women and their bodies.

Homosexuality split the young people in their views, gender being a significant difference, where it is clearly young men who felt obliged to 'protect' their own (hetero) sexuality, or 'police' that of others, through the expression of homophobic attitudes. The young women, while showing some homophobia and almost seeming to enjoy voicing their fears of 'predatory' lesbians, were in general much more accommodating to a liberal stance on homosexuality. Some of the young people, generally the older ones, were beginning to express more interest in what homosexuality might mean. Rather than simply expressing homophobia, they had some insights into the nature of 'difference'; and begin to endorse an individual's right to choice over sexuality, as they did in other areas of life.[6]

The moral debates around these issues show a pattern of sexual values that can be fiercely contested, through the varying backgrounds of culture, class and community, with gender as a vital component running through most if not all these debates. As issues that cause debate and disagreement in the wider popular discourse, they are also ones that would benefit from airing within sex and relationships education programmes.

---

6   A more detailed account of these young people's views on homosexuality can be found in Sharpe, 2002.

5. Engaging with young people's sexual values

Debates over sex and relationships education frequently wrestle over the 'moral message' that should be conveyed to young people. For example, materials are derided both for being 'value free' and for 'promoting' particular agendas or identities. Both sides of this debate share a misapprehension that young people are in some sense morally incompetent, simply waiting for guidance as to what is right and what is wrong. Developmental perspectives on the acquisition of moral identities tend to assume a linear process, whereby over time young people go through a number of stages of moral development, characterised by increasing complexity. As we have seen, young people's sexual values do change over time, generally (but not always) becoming more flexible and complex. Yet the main problem with this developmental perspective is that young people are understood as moving towards moral competence, and never as having 'arrived'. What we hope to have conveyed through this thinkpiece is that young people enter the classroom as active moral agents, engaged with and implicated in complex and contradictory moral discourses and debates. This does not mean that they are clear or confident about their values, or that these values will stay the same over time.

We also hope to have shown that young people cannot simply be seen as a single group. Rather, they are positioned very differently in relation to class, age, gender, ethnicity, religion, locality and sexuality. Their moral views are both uniquely individual and defined in relation to wider collectivities such as family, neighbourhood and community. Again, the recognition of the importance of context when discussing sexual values tends to evaporate in the face of universalising discourses of development and morality. However, contemporary policy discourses of social inclusion and exclusion are founded on an implicit recognition of the relationship between local cultures and distinct sexual values. These policy frameworks can themselves be highly judgmental, valuing the middle-class values that may prioritise individual outcomes over working-class values that may prioritise care and the collective. Some readers may have found some of the young people's views presented here unsettling – and no doubt different readers will have been unsettled by different things. Our intention is not to celebrate young people's sexual values in a naïve manner. Rather we are interested in promoting an active engagement with them, one that assumes such morality as already existing. In our view it is crucial that the teaching of personal, social and health education (PSHE) and Citizenship provides a space for the expression and exploration of moral discourse, encouraging reflection, deliberation and dialogue. There are many points of learning that can be drawn from the research findings presented here with direct relevance to formal and informal educational settings.

Patterns and structures

Sexual values exist as part of wider structures of values and are shaped by age, gender, social class, religion and ethnicity. In exploring particular values issues, it may be worth considering how certain attitudes relate to other issues to form part of specific 'factors', as identified through the questionnaire research. We can do this through looking again at these factors, which were described in more detail in *Patterns in sexual values* on page 7, and are given in Figure 5.1.

So for example, issues in the 'sexual values factor' may be explored in relation to the strong gender divisions which were found to increase with age. Issues in the 'illicit conventions factor' could be explored in relation to the class distinctions which found greater disapproval among middle-class young people. And in the 'life issues factor' subjects like abortion may be explored primarily in relation to age, religiosity and class. Young people from a middle-class background were more accepting than those from a working-class background. Finally, the issues within the 'trust and interpersonal values factor' may be explored in relation to age and the peaking of disapproval found in Years 7 and 8.

Values regimes

In exploring the ways in which young people distinguish between 'good' and 'bad' sex, we were able to identify a number of values regimes through which judgements are made over whether sex is legitimate or illegitimate. These were:

- Romance: Sex as legitimised by love

- Play: Sex as legitimised by pleasure

- Security: Sex as legitimised by commitment

Figure 5.1 Factors reflecting young people's values

Sexual values factor

Watching or reading pornography

Pressurising someone to have sex

Prostitution

Sexism

Unsafe sex

Illicit conventions factor

Using violence in self-defence

Carrying a weapon

Drinking alcohol

Taking revenge

Fighting

Sexual intercourse under the age of 16

Graffiti/spray-painting

Life issues factor

Suicide

Abortion

Euthanasia

Cloning animals

Trust and interpersonal values factor

Calling people names

Two-timing

Lying to your parents

Divorce

- Equity: Sex as legitimised by consent

- Legality: Sex as legitimised by the law

- Safety: Sex as legitimised by its consequences

Some of these regimes are highly gendered. For example girls are more likely to legitimise sex through love, and boys through pleasure. The burdens of sexual safety are more likely to fall onto the shoulders of girls, while the work of ascertaining consent appears to fall to young men who are constructed as having greater sexual agency. By making these values regimes explicit to young people and encouraging them to explore the possibilities of moving between these regimes in making judgements, it may be possible both to encourage dialogue and to develop reflexivity.

Debates

Each of the areas of debate identified in the thinkpiece represents an arena in which sexual values are contested between young people. In considering the implications for practice, this thinkpiece offers us new ways of approaching work on sex and relationships with young people. For example instead of engaging in discussions of whether homosexuality is right or wrong when discussing prejudice, it may be more beneficial to explore whether it is just and fair to treat people disrespectfully and to look at the moral issues around sexual identity and individual choice. Likewise, in discussing sexual activity or teenage pregnancy instead of trying to 'convince' young people it is not a good idea to have sex or become a parent early, it may be more helpful to explore the influences on decision-making and the help and support a young person would need. Most of all, perhaps, it reminds us that we need to consider and address what it feels like to be young. Underneath the outward expression of their values, young people have strong feelings based on their experiences and those of their family and friends. Trying to force or prescribe universal values will not be helpful, rather it is more helpful to work with young people in ways that develop dialogue and reflection in these areas, although it must be recognised that work needs to be undertaken to make such discussions as 'safe' as possible.

The effective use of distancing techniques, which allow young people to explore and discuss authentic scenarios that are like them but not them, enable such safety to be developed in both formal and informal education settings. As is reflected in this research, young people are able to, and enjoy, discussing 'moral' issues and have much to say and learn from the process. With an increasing emphasis on citizenship and active participation in schools and the community, the commitment to engaging young people in moral, topical and social issues is greater than ever before.

References

Bragg, S and Buckingham, D (2002) *Young People and Sexual Content on Television: A review of research.* London: BBC.

Connell, R (1995) *Masculinities.* London: Polity Press.

Douglas, N, Warwick, I, Kemp, S and Whitty, G (1997*) Playing it Safe: Responses of secondary school teachers to lesbian and gay pupils, bullying, HIV and AIDS education, and Section 28.* London: Terence Higgins Trust.

Epstein, D 'Keeping them in their place: Hetero/sexist harassment, gender and the enforcement of heterosexuality', in Adkins, L and Holland, J (eds) (1996) *Sexualising the Social.* Basingstoke: Macmillan.

Epstein, D (1997) 'Boyz' own stories: Masculinities and sexualities in school', *Gender and Education,* 9, 1, 105–116.

Epstein, D and Johnson, R (1998) *Schooling Sexualities.* Buckingham: Open University Press.

Forrest, S, Biddle, G and Clift, S (1997) *Talking About Homosexuality in the Secondary School.* Horsham: AVERT.

Frosh, S, Phoenix, A and Pattman, R (2001) *Young Masculinities.* Basingstoke: Palgrave.

Giddens, A (1992) *The Transformation of Intimacy: Sexuality, love and eroticism in modern societies.* Cambridge: Polity Press.

Giddens, A (1999) *The Reith Lectures.* London: BBC.

Hawkes, Gail, 'Liberalising heterosexuality', in Allen, G (ed) (1999), *The Sociology of the Family: A reader.* Oxford: Blackwell.

Hey, V (1997) *The Company She Keeps: An ethnography of girls' friendships.* Buckingham: Open University Press.

Hilton, G (2003) *Listening to the Boys Again: An exploration of what boys want to learn in sex education classes and how they want to be taught.* Paper given at the Sex/Sexuality and Relationships Education Conference, 29 May 2003, Institute of Education, University of London.

Holland, J, Ramazanoglu, C and Sharpe, S (1993*) Wimp or Gladiator: Contradictions in acquiring male sexuality.* WRAP Paper 7, London: The Tufnell Press.

Holland, J, Ramazanoglu, C, Sharpe, S and Thomson, R (1998) *The Male in the Head: Young people, heterosexuality and power.* London: The Tufnell Press.

Johnson, A, Wadsworth, J, Wellings, K and Field, J (1994) *Sexual Attitudes and Lifestyle.* Oxford: Blackwell.

Jones, G (2002) *The Youth Divide: Diverging paths to adulthood*. Bristol/York: The Policy Press/Joseph Rowntree Foundation.

Kehily, M (1999) 'More Sugar? Teenage magazines and sexuality', *Sex Education Matters*, 9 (Summer), 7–8.

Kehily, M (2002) *Sexuality, Gender and Schooling: Shifting agendas in social learning*. London: Routledge.

Lees, S (1986) *Losing Out: Sexuality and adolescent girls*. London: Hutchinson.

Lees, S (1993) *Sugar and Spice: Sexuality and adolescent girls*. London: Penguin.

Mac An Ghaill, M (1994) *The Making of Men*. Buckingham: Open University Press.

McGrellis, S, Henderson, S, Holland, J, Sharpe, S and Thomson, R (2000*) Through the Moral Maze: A quantitative study of young people's moral values*. London: The Tufnell Press.

Measor, L, Tiffin, C and Miller, K (2000) *Young People's Views on Sex Education: Education, attitudes and behaviour*. London: RoutledgeFalmer.

Moore, S and Rosenthal, D 'Adolescent sexual behaviour' in Roker, D and Coleman, J (eds) (1998) *Teenage Sexuality: Health, risks and education*. Reading: Harwood Academic.

Nayak, A and Kehily, M (1996) 'Playing it Straight: Masculinities, homophobias and schooling', *Journal of Gender Studies*, 5, 2, 211–230.

O'Donnell, M and Sharpe, S (2000) *Uncertain Masculinities: Youth, ethnicity and class in contemporary Britain*. London: Routledge.

Scott, S, Jackson, S and Backett-Milburn, K (1998) 'Swings and roundabouts: Risk anxiety in the everyday worlds of children', *Sociology*, 32, 4, 689–707.

Sharpe, S (1987) *Falling for Love: Teenage mothers talk*. London: Virago.

Sharpe, S (1976, 1994) *Just Like a Girl: How girls learn to be women*. Harmondsworth: Penguin.

Sharpe, S (2001) *More Than Just a Piece of Paper? Young people's views on marriage and relationships*. London: National Children's Bureau.

Sharpe, S (2002) '"It's really hard to come to terms with": Young people's views on homosexuality', *Sex Education*, 2, 3, 263–277.

Smith, T (1993) 'Influence of socio-economic factors on attaining targets for reducing teenage pregnancies', *British Medical Journal*, 306, 1232–1235.

Thomson, R 'It was the way we were watching it: young men's accounts of pornography' in Hearn, J and Roseneil, S (eds) (1999) *Consuming Cultures: Power and resistance*. London: Macmillan.

Thomson, R (2000) 'Dream on: The logic of sexual practice', *Journal of Youth Studies*, 3, 4, 407–427.

Waites, M (2003) 'Equality at last? Homosexuality, heterosexuality and the age of consent in the United Kingdom', *Sociology*, 37.

Waites, M (forthcoming, 2005) The Fixity of Sexual Identities in the Public Sphere: Biomedical knowledge, liberalism and the heterosexual/homosexual binary in late modernity, sexualities.

Warwick, I and Douglas, N (2000*) Safe for All: A best practice guide to prevent homophobic bullying in schools*. London: Citizenship 21.

Weeks, J (1989) *Sex, Politics and Society: The regulation of sexuality since 1800*. London: Longman.

Wellings, K and others (2001) 'Sexual behaviour in Britain: early heterosexual experience', *The Lancet*, 358, 1843–1850.

Index

Available from NCB Book Sales

More Than Just a Piece of Paper? Young people's views on marriage and relationships

Sue Sharpe

How should we teach about marriage in a way that is relevant to young people? This refreshing book explores young people's views on marriage and divorce and engages with new research on the changing family and couple relationships.

2001. 80pp. ISBN 1 900990 65 2. Price £10.95. NCB members £7.95

From Fear to Respect. Young people's views on violence

Sue Sharpe

From Fear to Respect examines violence in the family; bullying; fighting; community violence; and violence in the media. It explores what legitimates such violence for young people; how young people's moral values about the rights and wrongs of violence clash with their life experiences; and how their attitudes and views may be the same or different from those of adults.

2004. 112pp. ISBN 1 904787 06 1. Price £14.00. NCB members £10.00

Faith, Values and Sex & Relationships Education

Simon Blake and Zarine Katrak

This book outlines approaches and strategies for developing effective sex and relationships education policy and practice in a multi-faith and multi-cultural society.

2002. 100pp. ISBN 1 900990 32 6. Price £12.00. NCB members £9.00

Sex, Alcohol and Other Drugs. Exploring the links in young people's lives

Jeanie Lynch and Simon Blake

For young people, sexual activity and the use of alcohol and other drugs are entwined. Drawing heavily on the perspectives of young people, professionals and research, *Sex, Alcohol and Other Drugs* provides a much needed foundation for developing policy and practice that is relevant to young people's lives and addresses the issues in a holistic fashion.

2004. 95pp. ISBN 1 904787 09 6. Price £14.00. NCB members £10.00

To order:

- post your order to Book Sales, National Children's Bureau, 8 Wakley Street, London EC1V 7QE
- fax your order to 020 7843 6087
- phone 020 7843 6029/8 to order by credit/debit card

For orders up to £28 add £4 for p&p. For orders £28 and over, add 15% of the total order for p&p. For orders below £28, please include payment with order.